THE ROUND THE WORLD QUIZ BOOK

SUE McMILLAN

THE ROUND THE WORLD QUIZ BOOK

Lonely Planet Kids

ACKNOWLEDGMENTS

Publishing Director	Piers Pickard
Publisher	Tim Cook
Commissioning Editor	Jen Feroze
Author	Sue McMillan
Designer	Hayley Warnham
Print production	Larissa Frost, Nigel Longuet

With thanks to: Jennifer Dixon

Lonely Planet Offices

Australia
The Malt Store, Level 3, 551 Swanston St, Carlton, Victoria, 3053 Australia
T: 03 8379 8000

IRELAND
Unit E, Digital Court, The Digital Hub, Rainsford St., Dublin 8

USA
124 Linden St., Oakland, CA 94607
T: 510 250 6400

UK
240 Blackfriars Road, London, SE1 8NW
T: 020 3771 5100

STAY IN TOUCH
lonelyplanet.com/contact

Published in April 2017 by Lonely Planet Global Ltd
CRN: 554153
ISBN: 978 1 78657 432 9
www.lonelyplanetkids.com
© Lonely Planet 2017
Printed in China

10 9 8 7 6 5 4 3 2 1

Paper in this book is certified against the Forest Stewardship Council™ standards. FSC™ promotes environmentally responsible, socially beneficial and economically viable management of the world's forests.

MIX
Paper from responsible sources
FSC™ C021741

CONTENTS

HOW TO USE THIS BOOK

How much do you know about the world? Are you confident about continents and in the know about oceans, or does your world knowledge need a little polishing? There's only one way to find out, so get ready to embark on the Round-the-World Quiz!

The questions in this book are divided into three different levels: Newbie, Rookie, and Genius. Each one is a bit trickier than the last, and each one is worth a point. Start at Newbie level and see how you do, then challenge yourself to answer the harder questions. Don't leave the rest of the family out, – why not ask Mom and Dad to tackle some Genius-level questions and see how much they really know?

Every question is worth one point. For questions where you have to match things up, such as the Newbie question on page 10, you have a chance to earn some bonus points, as each item correctly matched is also worth a point.

Remember: You don't have to answer every question on each page, so don't worry if you get stuck.

At the back of the book you'll find a map of the world. Your mission is to score enough points to color it all in.

Each area of the map is labeled with a number. Once you score that number of points, you can color the area in. The more questions you answer, the faster you will color your map!

So, get your colored pencils ready, get your brain in gear, and set off on the Round-the-World Quiz...

AMAZING LOCATIONS

CONTINENT CONUNDRUM

Let's start the quiz by checking out our planet's continents – your round-the-world journey starts here...

NEWBIE

Can you correctly name each of the continents on the map?

Europe

Asia

Africa

Oceania

Antarctica

North America

South America

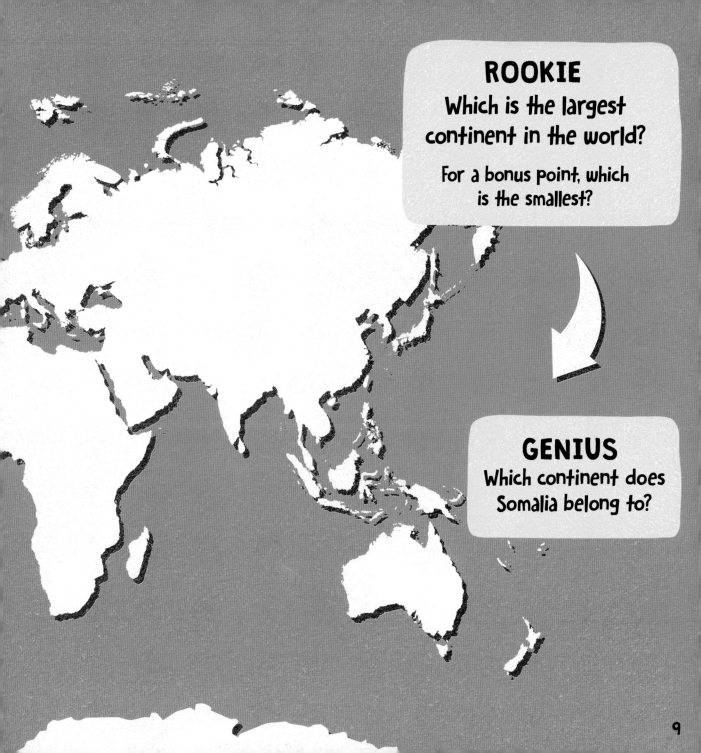

ROOKIE
Which is the largest
continent in the world?

For a bonus point, which
is the smallest?

GENIUS
Which continent does
Somalia belong to?

9

FLYING THE FLAG

Here are the outlines of five national flags, with a description under each.
Can you match the country with the correct flag?

1. FRANCE   2. BHUTAN   3. CANADA   4. USA   5. JAPAN

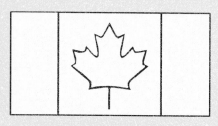

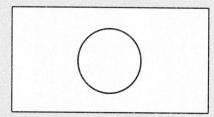

A) The 50 stars on this flag represent each of its 50 member states. It's sometimes called the "Stars and Stripes" or "Old Glory."

B) This flag has vertical bands of red, white, and red, with a red maple leaf in the middle. Unsurprisingly, it's sometimes known as the "Maple Leaf"!

C) This is a simple flag design, made up of a red circle on a white background. It is known as the "Hinomaru," which means "Circle of the Sun."

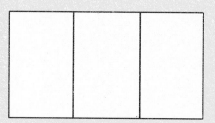

D) This flag has vertical bands in blue, white, and red. It is known as the "Tricolore."

E) This flag is made up of two triangles in different colors, overlaid by a picture of the mythical thunder dragon.

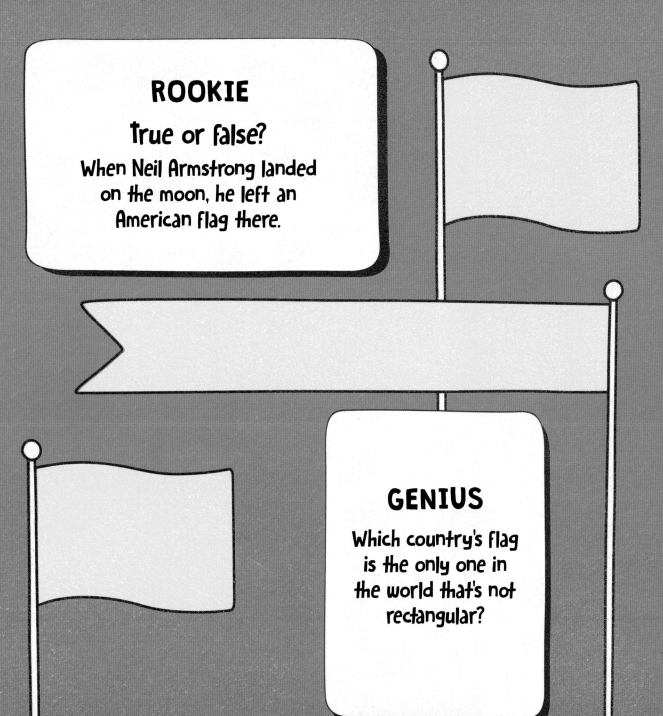

ROOKIE

True or false?

When Neil Armstrong landed on the moon, he left an American flag there.

GENIUS

Which country's flag is the only one in the world that's not rectangular?

COUNTRY QUERIES

There are seven European countries hidden in the word search. Can you find them all?

```
C E A O I K A L I Y Q K F E Z M
I R C G A D G E S P A I N S I N
A I N O R W A Y I A N G U S A I
R E B A R Y N F A P K G N O S P
S G E R M A N Y O R E N T I N O
N I S O O F Y M I R S A A Y P B
D N L B H T A H V I R A K L E C
O A N C D H T I E S E C N A R F
E E A E O E C P C R I L Y T I T
C B R N H D L I Y L T L N I R I
E B E R E E I A D A N E G E D A
E I N S F I N L A N D H A E O Z
R R I B O R P A Z C L P N N N F
G A E M O N I Z W T T U A L M O
M C S N A I D N I I A D T U H N
```

Finland

Norway

Germany

France

Italy

Spain

Greece

For a bonus point, which of these countries is the largest?

ROOKIE

Most countries in the world are famous for certain things. For example, Belgium is really well-known for its amazing chocolate, yum!

Take a look at the lists for five countries below. On each list there's one thing that the country isn't known for. Can you find each one?

Australia
the Outback, kangaroos, the Great Wall, crocodiles, the Great Barrier Reef

Canada
Niagara Falls, bears, lakes, ice hockey, silk, maple syrup

Italy
the Leaning Tower of Pisa, the Terracotta Army, St. Mark's Square, pasta, the Sistine Chapel

United Kingdom
Stonehenge, Big Ben, the Forbidden City, the Queen, the White Cliffs of Dover

United States
Hollywood, the White House, giant pandas, the Empire State Building, baseball

GENIUS

Look at the five items you've selected in the Rookie question. Can you name the country that's famous for all of these?

WHERE ON EARTH...?

People travel for thousands of miles to see some of these famous landmarks, but do you know where you will find them? Let's find out!

A) the Taj Mahal

B) the Statue of Liberty

1. Agra, India
2. Giza, Egypt
3. New York, USA
4. Paris, France
5. Rome, Italy
6. Sydney, Australia
7. London, United Kingdom

C) the Colosseum

F) Tower Bridge

D) the Eiffel tower

E) the Pyramids

G) the Opera House

true or false?

The Statue of Liberty was given to the United States by Canada.

GENIUS

At one of the tourist spots on the opposite page, you can also see an ancient statue that has the head of a man and the body of a lion. It's called the Sphinx, but where would you have to go to see it?

TERRIFIC TRANSPORTATION

Ding, ding! All aboard to see if you can answer these tricky transportation questions:

NEWBIE

Can you fill in the blanks?

- In London, getting around is easy if you jump on a bright .... (blue / red / green) double-decker bus.

- New York is famous for its .... (pink / purple / yellow) taxis.

- In Venice, a popular way to travel on the canals is by .... (gondola / bathtub / yacht)

- In Amsterdam, many people choose to see the sights by .... (cycling / hopping / jogging)

- In Japan, you can travel at speeds of over 200mph (320kph) on the .... (bullet / tortoise / creeping) train.

ROOKIE

1. Match the city with the correct name for its underground railway, then answer the multiple-choice questions opposite:

Paris   New York   London

Subway   Underground (or Tube)   Metro

2. In Moscow, Russia, the subway system is unusual because:

A) it's not underground!
B) some stations are incredibly beautiful, with marble ceilings and even chandeliers
C) travel is free
D) all the trains are double-decker

3. The Japanese subway system has workers who:

A) tell people off for using a cell phone
B) give travelers free manicures
C) fine anyone who eats on the trains
D) push people onto the trains during rush hour

GENIUS

The longest train line in the world is the Trans-Siberian railway from Moscow to Vladivostock, but just how long a journey is it?

5,772 miles (9,289km)   637 miles (1,025km)

264 miles (425km)   78 miles (125km)

17

CITY SEARCH

NEWBIE

There are 11 cities hidden in this word search. Can you find them all?

O	U	A	O	I	K	A	N	D	E	N	V	E	R	Z	M
C	P	C	G	A	D	G	E	S	K	A	I	N	S	I	N
S	S	A	H	A	A	G	W	D	A	L	L	A	S	A	I
I	A	B	A	R	Y	N	Y	A	P	K	G	N	O	S	P
C	N	Q	R	M	A	N	O	O	R	E	N	T	I	N	O
N	G	S	O	D	A	L	R	I	R	S	A	A	R	P	B
A	T	L	A	N	T	A	K	V	I	R	A	K	L	E	N
R	L	O	S	A	N	G	E	L	E	S	S	N	A	R	O
F	E	A	I	O	E	C	P	C	R	I	L	Y	T	I	T
N	F	R	N	C	D	L	I	Y	E	L	T	T	A	E	S
A	B	E	R	E	A	I	O	D	A	N	E	G	E	D	O
S	I	N	S	V	A	G	Y	M	R	A	H	A	E	O	B
R	R	I	B	O	R	P	K	Z	C	H	I	C	A	G	O
G	A	E	M	O	N	I	O	W	T	T	U	A	L	M	O
W	A	S	H	I	N	G	T	O	N	D	C	T	U	H	N

New York
Washington, DC
Chicago
Seattle
Boston
Los Angeles
Dallas
Tokyo
San Francisco
Atlanta
Denver

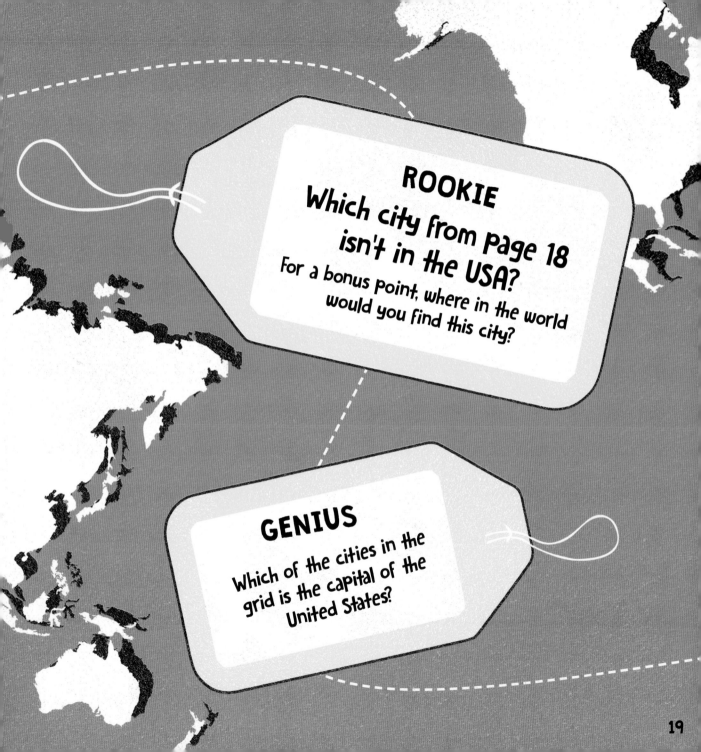

ROOKIE
Which city from page 18 isn't in the USA?
For a bonus point, where in the world would you find this city?

GENIUS
Which of the cities in the grid is the capital of the United States?

19

TOWERING PLACES

Unscramble the words to finish these sentences.

Burj Khalifa, the world's tallest skyscraper, has so much glass that it takes 36 workers three NOTMSH to clean the windows!

Taiwan's Taipei 101 has the world's fastest ROVELETSA, which reach speeds of more than 37mph (60kph).

The Empire State Building in New York was the first skyscraper to have more than 100 FOROLS.

The Petronas Towers in Malaysia are the world's tallest WITN towers.

At the top of Toronto's CN Tower, visitors can stand on a LAGSS floor, if they dare!

ROOKIE

What's the name of the tallest building in London, UK?

A) the Shard
B) the Point
C) the Heights
D) the Tower

GENIUS

Burj Khalifa is how many times taller than Egypt's Great Pyramid of Giza?

A) two
B) three
C) four and a half
D) more than five

OUTSTANDING BUILDINGS

1. Which one of these buildings would need an elevator?

A) a ranch
B) a skyscraper
C) a house
D) a shed

2. If you were going to build a super-tall building, would you make it from:

A) straw
B) mud
C) bricks
D) steel

3. Which one of these buildings is the official residence of the president of the USA? Is it the:

A) Gray House
B) White House
C) Green House
D) Red House

4. The world's first "skyscraper," the Home Insurance Building in Chicago, was built in 1885. How many floors did it have when it first opened?

A) 8 floors
B) 50 floors
C) 10 floors

5. Things moved quickly with skyscrapers. When the Empire State Building went up in New York in 1931, it had:

A) 92 floors
B) 65 floors
C) 102 floors

How many rooms are
there in London's Buckingham Palace?

A) 775
B) 157
C) 36
D) 12

GENIUS

If the elevators were out of
service in Burj Khalifa, the
world's tallest tower, how
many stairs would you have
to climb?

A) 215   C) 2,900
B) 1,970   D) 740

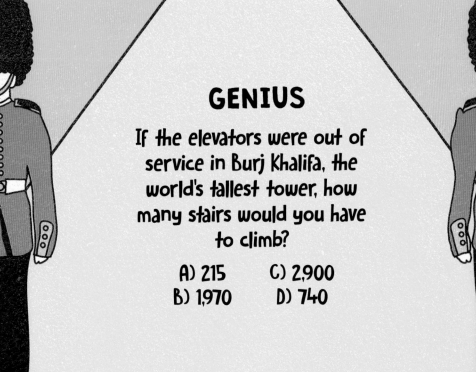

GETTING AWAY FROM IT ALL

Read these five travel reviews – can you figure out
who has been where from their descriptions?

← → ↻   **NEWBIE**

1. This was my first trip to Europe. We cycled, and had pancakes for lunch. Best of all was our trip to the countryside to see the fields of tulips – they were so colorful!

2. Wow! I feel so lucky to have been to Africa. We went out in a jeep and saw lions, leopards, buffalo, rhinos and elephants. It was really hot, but totally amazing!

3. Yesterday we went out to the reef in a boat. Everyone looked funny walking in their flippers! The sea is so clear that we saw loads of fish underwater. I even spotted a shipwreck!

4. Just had the best day ever! Loads of epic rides – I'm still dizzy from Deathly Descent. I loved the water park, too. Check out the Funnel of Fear – it's awesome!

5. The Rockies are so cool. We've been hiking, cycled along the trails, and gone rock climbing. We've seen loads of wildlife – including some black bears, so we've had to be super-careful with food and make sure that we clean up our trash.

- diving in the Bahamas
- camping in a national park in Colorado
- on safari in Kenya
- theme park in Florida
- a short break in Holland

ROOKIE

One of the reviews mentions roller coasters. The world's fastest roller coaster, Ferrari World's Formula Rossa in the United Arab Emirates, reaches what at its top speed?

A) 62mph (100kph)
B) 93mph (150kph)
C) 118mph (190kph)
D) 149mph (240kph)

GENIUS

Another review mentions storing food if you are camping near bears. Should you:

A) store it in your tent with you
B) put it in a secure container
C) leave it on a picnic table and hope the bears don't eat it

INCREDIBLE PLACES

There are so many sights around the world
that will take your breath away, from thundering waterfalls to colorful
coral reefs and towering mountains. Let's begin with a quiz to see how much
you know about some of nature's most incredible places...

NEWBIE

Unscramble the words to finish these sentences.

1. At 29,000 feet (8,848 m), Mount VERESTE is the tallest mountain
in the world.

2. The ARDNG CYONNA is more than 1 mile (1.6km) deep in places.

3. The TRAEG IRERARB FREE can be seen from outer space.

4. VCIROTAI LLSAF is also known as "the smoke that thunders" because
of the noise and mist that the water creates as it tumbles
into the gorge below.

ROOKIE

1. Paricutin is a .... that formed in 1943. In nine years, it grew to a height of 1,400 ft (424 m).

A) volcano
B) cliff
C) waterfall

2. The harbor at Rio de Janeiro in Brazil is the largest natural .... in the world.

A) reef
B) island
C) bay

3. During the Aurora Borealis, curtains of color appear in the sky. It is also called the ....

A) Northern Brights
B) Northern Lights
C) Northern Surprise

GENIUS

Here's a list of five of the Seven Wonders of the Ancient World. Can you spot which two are missing?

– Colossus of Rhodes
– Statue of Zeus at Olympia
– Lighthouse of Alexandria
– Temple of Artemis at Ephesus
– Mausoleum at Halicarnassus

For an extra point – which one of these two missing wonders can still be seen today?

COOL CONTINENTS

Can you match each of the continents with the fact about it?

NEWBIE

1. Europe

2. Asia

3. South America

4. North America

5. Africa

6. Oceania

7. Antarctica

A) You'll find the Amazon rainforest here.

B) Take a trip here if you dare! There's nothing but ice for miles and miles!

C) This continent is home to the Sahara, the largest hot desert in the world.

D) Made up of one big island and lots of smaller island countries, this continent is found in the Pacific Ocean.

E) This huge continent includes freezing Alaska, the Great Lakes, and the baking heat of Death Valley.

F) Almost half the world's people live on this massive continent.

G) Here you can visit cities, winter ski resorts, and Mediterranean beaches, but you won't find any deserts!

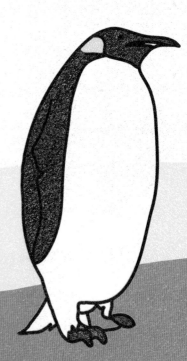

ROOKIE
true or false?
Kangaroos and many other animals and plants that live in Australia are not found anywhere else in the world.

GENIUS
true or false?
In winter months, Antarctica almost doubles in size.

WADE INTO RIVERS

Hope you've packed your canoe; it's time to plunge into some of the world's most amazing rivers!

NEWBIE

1. The longest river in the world, which flows for an incredible 4,132 miles (6,650km), is:

A) the Nile
B) the Amazon
C) the Mississippi
D) the Thames

2. The Congo River in Africa is the deepest in the world. In places its depth is:

A) 52 feet (16 m) – that's about the same as a two-story house
B) 220 feet (67 m) – that's a little more than the height of London's Tower Bridge
C) 722 feet (220 m) – that's about the same height as the towers on San Francisco's Golden Gate Bridge!
D) 66 feet (20 m) – that's almost as much as six school buses stacked one on top of the other

3. The Amazon River in South America is home to:

A) pink dolphins
B) meat-eating piranhas (fish)
C) electric eels
D) all of the above

4. The Roe in Montana, USA, is the shortest river in the world. It flows for a puny:

A) 200 feet (61 m) – that's about the same length as six school buses end to end
B) 630 feet (192 m) – that's about the same as the wingspan of a jumbo jet
C) 325 feet (99 m) – that's nearly the length of a soccer field
D) 417 feet (127 m) – that's about the same length as six railroad cars

5. The Huang He in China is also known as the:

A) Mother River
B) Yellow River
C) Cradle of China's Civilization
D) all of the above

ROOKIE

In the 1960s, the Cuyahoga River in Ohio, USA, was so polluted that it...

A) went frothy, like a bubble bath
B) turned bright red
C) smelled like rotten eggs
D) caught fire – 12 times!

GENIUS

In Germany, the Danube river is sometimes known as "The Blue Danube." This is also the name of a piece of music composed by Johann Strauss in 1866. What type of dance would you do to this music?

A) break dancing
B) a waltz
C) a jive
D) a tango

CONQUERING MOUNTAINS

From towering snowcapped peaks to smoldering volcanoes, mountains are marvelous. But how's your knowledge? Can you conquer these questions, or will you get stranded at base camp? Let's find out!

NEWBIE

```
M S G E L B R U S E N V A R Z I
C P V V A D G E S K A I R S I N
S G M E A W G W D A L L I S A I
I A V R R S N G G P K G N W S O
C N Q E M A N M O R V N T M N R
M G S S D A L R Z R I I A R P A
U T V T P R C S C I N A K L E J
R L D S A N N E L F S S D A R N
F E A I O E C P C R O L Y T I A
N F R N T D L I Y E N T T A E M
A B E S E D I O D E N A L I D I
S I R S V A G Y M R A H A E O L
R A I B O R P K Z C H I C A G I
C A E F O N I O W T T U A G M K
A C O N C A G U A M D C T U H D
```

The Seven Summits is a list of the tallest mountains on each of the seven continents. Mountains aren't usually difficult to spot, but can you find their names in this word search?

Everest (Asia)

Aconcagua (South America)

Denali (North America)

Kilimanjaro (Africa)

Elbrus (Europe)

Vinson (Antarctica)

Carstensz (Oceania)

ROOKIE

Which is taller, Mauna Kea or Mount Everest?

GENIUS

True or false? Earth's mountains are the largest in our solar system.

UNDER A WATERFALL

Whether they're huge thundering sheets or tall narrow ribbons – waterfalls are wonderful. But how much do you know about them? Let's find out!

NEWBIE

True or false?

1. Waterfalls can be used to generate electricity.

2. At nighttime, the water flowing over Niagara Falls is turned off.

3. Waterfalls never freeze.

ROOKIE

Here are five waterfalls and some fabulous facts. Can you match them up?

1. Victoria Falls, Zambia and Zimbabwe

2. Niagara Falls, Canada and USA

3. Iguacu Falls, Brazil and Argentina

4. Angel Falls, Venezuela

5. Khone Phapheng Falls, Laos

A) This waterfall is made up of 275 smaller falls. A special walkway gives visitors an amazing view, with water tumbling around them on almost every side.

B) At 3,211 feet (979 m), this is the tallest waterfall in the world. It is so high that in summer a lot of the water turns to mist before it hits the bottom!

C) This waterfall is visited by over 30 million people a year. Many travel close to the bottom of the falls on a boat called the *Maid of the Mist*.

D) This waterfall forms a series of rapids on the Mekong River. The water is so powerful that boats can't use this stretch of the river.

E) The roar from this waterfall is so loud it can be heard up to 25 miles (40km) away.

GENIUS

Waterfalls have played host to some amazing stunts over the years. Three of these are true, so which one didn't happen?

A) Jimmie Angel crashed a plane at Angel Falls, which were named after him.
B) Heza Lira went over Iguacu Falls in a canoe.
C) Annie Edson Taylor went over Niagara Falls in a barrel.
D) Lukas Irmler and Reinhard Kleindl walked across a tightrope over Victoria Falls.

EXPLORING A RAINFOREST

Rainforests are often called "the lungs of the Earth" because the trees produce much of the oxygen that we need to breathe. Take a deep breath and see how many of these rainforest questions you can answer:

```
M A D A G A S C A R N V A R Z N
C P A L A Y E R S K A I R S I I
S G M K A W G W D A L Z I S A S
I A P A P U A N E W G U I N E A
C O N S E R V A T I O N T M N B
M G S S D N L R Z R I I A R P R
U T V O O L C S D A I N T R E E
R L D Z A A N E L F S S R A R V
F E A I C C C P C R O L E O I I
N M R N T I L I Y E N T E A E R
A B E S E P I O D E N A S I D O
S I E S V O G Y M R A I A E O G
R A I B O R P K K C H I C A G N
C M O U N T K I N A B U L U M O
A C E N D A N G E R E D T U H C
```

Find the rainforests and rainforest words in the grid:

Amazon

Congo River Basin

Daintree

Mount Kinabulu

Papua New Guinea

Madagascar

trees

tropical

layers

conservation

endangered

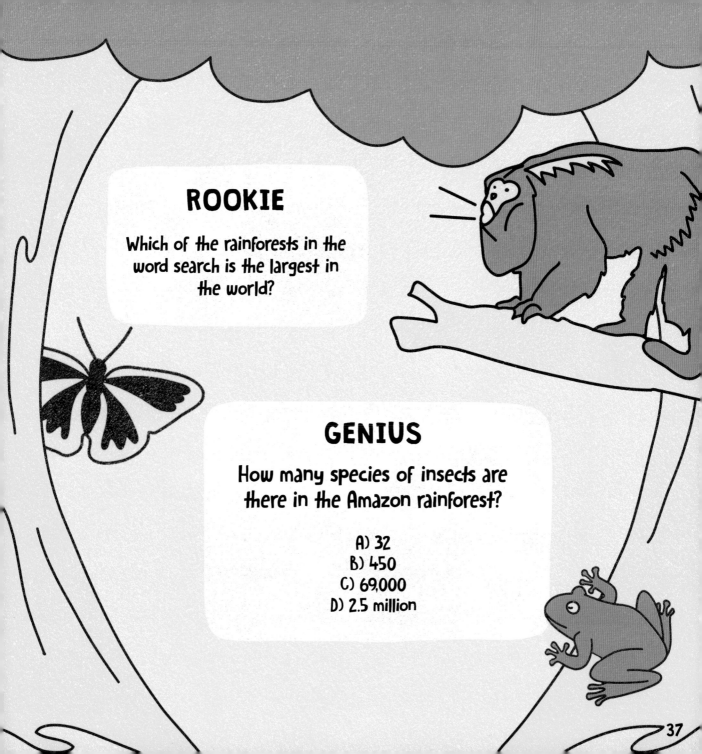

ROOKIE

Which of the rainforests in the word search is the largest in the world?

GENIUS

How many species of insects are there in the Amazon rainforest?

A) 32
B) 450
C) 69,000
D) 2.5 million

CROSSING DESERTS

It's time to visit some of Earth's most inhospitable places – let's see how much YOU know about deserts, if you dare!

NEWBIE

See if you can choose the right answer from the list below:

1. What is a desert?
A) something sweet you have at the end of a meal
B) a harsh place where there is very little rainfall or snow
C) a hot, dry place full of sand

2. True or false?
Antarctica is a desert.

3. Hot deserts such as the Sahara sizzle during the day, but at night what temperatures do they reach?

A) a freezing 32°F (0°C)
B) a chilly 50°F (10°C)
C) a sticky 86°F (30°C)

ROOKIE

There are six deserts in the list of place names below – see if you can spot them all.

New York
Milan
Sahara
Paris
Arabian
London
Atacama
Rome
Gobi
Mojave
Kalahari
Rio de Janeiro
Toronto
Sydney

GENIUS
True or false?

1. Deserts cover about a fifth of the Earth's land surface.
2. All deserts are covered in sand.
3. The Sahara Desert spans 12 countries.
4. It never snows in deserts.
5. Sandboarding is a sport similar to snowboarding, which is done on sand dunes.

DIVE INTO LAKES

Whether they're big, small, freshwater, or saltwater, lakes are lovely. But how much do you know? Can you make a splash, or is your lake knowledge lacking?

1. Unscramble the names of these five freshwater lakes in North America:

SUPRORIE   EEIR
OARTNIO   MIAIGNCH
HUNOR

2. Together they are known as the:

A) Green Lakes
B) Tiny Lakes
C) Great Lakes

ROOKIE

Finish these lake sentences by choosing the correct word to fill in the blank:

1. Baikal is the world's .... (oldest / youngest / smallest) lake.

2. It's estimated that Canada has around two .... (hundred / thousand / million) lakes – more than any other country in the world!

3. Loch Ness in Scotland and Lake Erie in Canada are both rumored to have .... (monsters / treasure / pirates) hiding in their waters.

4. Ninety percent of the Aral Sea is now .... (desert / salty / polluted) because rivers that fed it have been diverted.

5. The Dead Sea is one of the world's most famous lakes because it's saltier than the ocean, which means that when you get in the water you .... (sink / float / shrivel)!

GENIUS

How much of the world's freshwater is stored in the five lakes from the Newbie question?

A) 0.5%   C) 17%
B) 4%   D) 20%

Bonus question

True or false?
Lakes do not have beaches.

MIND-BLOWING NATURE

Nature has created some incredible sights all over the world. Some are so strange they can't possibly be true. Or can they? Prepare to have your mind blown...

NEWBIE

Can you unscramble the words to find out what's special about some of nature's greatest hits?

1. In the Sounding Sand Desert, Mongolia, the DNWI makes an eerie noise like a car engine whining.

2. Lake Hillier in Australia is unusual because the water is PKNI, thanks to its high salt levels and the algae that live there.

3. In Death Valley, California, the "sailing stones" have mystified people for years because they seem to MVOE on their own!

4. The island of Socotra in the Indian Ocean is known as the most IENLA place on Earth, thanks to its weird and wonderful plants, which aren't found anywhere else.

5. The waves have worn away the sand to leave RKCOS that are shaped like bowling balls on a beach in California.

ROOKIE

1. In Ireland, the Giant's Causeway is a:

A) wide ancient road that goes up and down lots of hills
B) series of rock columns that form stepping stones down from a cliff to the sea
C) path of stepping stones across a river

2. Table Mountain, in South Africa, gets its name because it:

A) was discovered by an explorer called Sir Edward Table
B) has a flat top, like a table
C) is green, like a pool table

3. In fall, New England in the USA is one of the best places to:

A) see the spectacular colors as the leaves turn from green to red, yellow, and orange
B) celebrate Halloween in style
C) eat pancakes with maple syrup

4. Old Faithful in Yosemite National Park is a geyser (a hole in the ground that shoots out hot water). It gets its name because it:

A) is predictable - eruptions happen every hour, so you are guaranteed to see it erupting with plumes of boiling water and steam
B) has not erupted for more than 300 years
C) erupts once a year, at Thanksgiving

5. In Sequoia National Park in California, people flock to visit "General Sherman":

A) a recently restored tank that was used in World War I
B) a gigantic tree more than 272 feet (83 m) tall and estimated to be more than 2,500 years old
C) a rare white squirrel that is sometimes seen darting between the enormous trees

Can you figure out which of these places is fake?

a) Chocolate Hills, Bohol Island, Philippines — more than 2,000 dome-shaped mounds that get their name because in the dry season, the grass turns brown, making them look like chocolate
b) Wave Rock, Australia — a sandstone formation 46 feet (14 m) high and around 360 feet (110 m) long, which looks just like a breaking wave
c) Jelly Sandwich Cliffs, Cornwall, UK — a famous seaside landmark which, thanks to its layers of white and pink rocks, looks just like a lunchtime snack

GENIUS

ANIMAL MAGIC

Earth is home to some incredible creatures. Let's explore the animal kingdom and see how much you know about our planet's beautiful beasts...

ANIMAL MYSTERIES

Unscramble the anagrams, and then see if you can match the animal names to their descriptions. Will you be king of the jungle?

NIOL   LETNAEHP   BAIBTR   NIENUGP   NEKAS   DIROLECOC

NEWBIE

1. I have scaly skin and a long body and tail. I lurk in rivers, and when animals come close, I snap them up with my powerful jaws, which are full of huge, pointy teeth!

2. I live in Africa, have a fearsome roar, and like to sleep in the sun. If I'm a male, I have a shaggy mane of hair around my face. If I'm a female, I hunt for food for the family.

3. I have a long narrow body like a worm, but I am much bigger. Listen for my hissing voice, and watch where you tread – you'll find me slithering along the ground. If I am in danger, I may bite!

4. I live in Antarctica – brrrr! I have a black back and a white tummy. Although I am a bird, I cannot fly. I'm great at swimming though, and catch lots of fish to eat.

5. I am small and furry, with long ears and a white fluffy tail. I live in a home called a burrow. If something scares me, I will scamper away, flashing my tail as I go.

6. I am the biggest land animal in the world. I have gray, wrinkled skin and a long trunk. When I call to the other animals in my herd, I make a trumpeting noise.

ROOKIE

Can you choose the correct group name for each of these animals?

1. A group of lions is called a

....

A) timid
B) pride
C) loud

2. A group of elephants is called a

....

A) herd
B) class
C) gang

3. A group of dolphins is called a

....

A) pod
B) dingle
C) nursery

4. A group of wolves is called a

....

A) party
B) pack
C) pile

5. A group of monkeys is called a

....

A) troop
B) gaggle
C) herd

GENIUS

True or false?

Some animals can freeze solid and survive.

INCREDIBLE INSECTS

There are far more creepy-crawlies than people on our planet. But how much do you know about them? See if you can match up these critters with their special features:

NEWBIE

1. spider
2. bee
3. butterfly
4. ladybug
5. glow worm

A) has delicate, pretty wings

B) has eight legs

C) has spots on its back

D) makes honey, yum!

E) can give off light from its rear end

ROOKIE

Many creepy-crawlies are harmless but some can give you a nasty nip. Use the clues to help you unscramble the words to find out their names.

1. If you annoy a WPSA, you may get a painful sting.

2. FEASL like hitching a ride on a cat or a dog, but their bites are itchy rather than painful.

3. Blood-sucking ICKST hop onto people and animals to feast on their blood. Yuck!

4. A bite from a STIQOUOM is annoying but watch out – in tropical countries, they can carry diseases.

5. A OSERHYFL makes a tiny cut in the skin so it can drink your blood. Yikes!

GENIUS

These beastly bugs take scary to a new level. See if you can correctly choose their secret weapons from the list below:

1. The poison arrow frog...

A) ...sprays poison from its mouth when it's threatened

B) ...eats poisonous bugs, which makes it poisonous to attackers

C) ...has long claws on its feet to defend itself

2. When it is attacked, the peanut bug...

A) ...can shed its tail and run away

B) ...sprays stinky-smelling liquid

C) ...can jump up to 7 feet (2 m) high to escape

3. The puss moth caterpillar...

A) ...shoots acid at anything that tries to eat it

B) ...has tiny poison-coated hairs on its back

C) ...can use its long tail spike to defend itself

EXCELLENT IMITATION

Animals have lots of ways of staying safe. Some pretend to be other things to fool their foes...

NEWBIE

Unscramble the words to find out how some animals stay safe.

1. The robber fly mimics the buzzing of a <u>EBE</u>.

2. The harmless milk snake protects itself by having <u>SSEPIRT</u> in the same colors as the Eastern coral snake, which has a nasty bite.

3. The owl butterfly has <u>YEE</u> spots and markings that make it look just like the bird it is named after.

4. The Atlas moth has a pattern on the edge of its wings that looks just like the head of a <u>NAKES</u> called a cobra.

5. <u>TICKS</u> insects look just like twigs to stay well hidden from attackers.

ROOKIE

True or false?
The caterpillar of the giant swallowtail butterfly looks just like a bird dropping.

GENIUS

True or false?
Fish are the only creatures that don't use mimicry to protect themselves.

HIDE AND SEEK!

Some animals fool others by hiding right in front of them. This is called camouflage.

All of these animals are real, except one. Can you find the fake one?

- The Glasswing butterfly's wings are see-through, just like glass!
- The leaf-tailed gecko has a tail that looks like an old dried leaf, so it's really hard to spot.
- The candy spider has a body that looks just like a shiny candy wrapper, so that animals think it is litter and leave it alone.
- The legs of the orchid mantis resemble the petals of an orchid, so it's really hard to spot it on the flowers.
- The longhorn beetle has stripes on its body that help it blend in with a tree trunk.

DANGER! DANGER!

There are plenty of animals that can be deadly dangerous, but can you tell a predator from a pussycat? Let's find out...

NEWBIE Can you spot these fearsome creatures in the grid below?

S	P	A	E	L	E	P	H	A	N	T	P	F	E	T	M
I	R	C	G	A	D	G	R	S	T	G	K	H	S	I	N
A	G	R	I	Z	Z	L	Y	B	E	A	R	U	S	G	R
R	E	B	A	R	Y	K	N	A	R	K	G	N	O	E	P
C	T	L	I	O	N	F	I	O	R	E	N	T	I	R	O
N	I	S	O	O	F	Y	M	I	A	S	A	A	C	P	B
G	R	E	A	T	W	H	I	T	E	S	H	A	R	K	A
E	A	N	C	D	H	T	K	E	B	C	Y	I	O	R	R
M	O	S	Q	U	I	T	O	C	R	I	L	Y	C	I	B
E	B	R	N	H	D	L	I	E	A	T	P	N	O	R	O
D	B	E	R	O	E	I	R	O	L	N	E	G	D	D	C
V	I	N	C	V	A	D	K	P	O	A	H	A	I	O	G
M	R	I	B	O	D	P	A	P	P	L	P	N	L	N	N
G	S	E	M	A	N	I	Z	I	T	T	U	A	E	M	I
C	E	S	N	A	I	D	N	H	I	A	D	T	U	H	K

lion

tiger

hippo

great white shark

polar bear

elephant

mosquito

king cobra

grizzly bear

crocodile

ROOKIE

In Africa, the hippo is more feared than the lion, as it has a terrible temper and is also very territorial – bad news if you happen to stray into its waters. But how long are its terrible tusks?

A) the same length as a newborn baby
B) as long as a banana
C) as long as a ballpoint pen

GENIUS
true or false?
the mosquito has killed more people than any of the other creatures on the word list on page 52.

53

PERILOUS POISON

Not all of nature's nasties are enormous with razor-sharp teeth. Some animals may be tiny, but they are just as scary, thanks to their deadly venom.

NEWBIE

Can you match the venomous creatures with the right description?

A) **SEA WASP**
B) **KOMODO DRAGON**
C) **REDBACK SPIDER**
D) **COASTAL TAIPAN SNAKE**
E) **POISON DART FROG**

1. I am about the size of a cherry tomato, and I am found in the rainforests of South America. My skin is covered in a poison so strong it could kill 10 people. My poison is used on arrow tips – that's how I get my name.

2. I am a giant lizard. I'm found in parts of Indonesia, and I have tough, scaly skin like armor. The venom from my bite isn't strong – it's my 60 teeth, which are covered in deadly germs, that cause the most damage! Yuck!

3. Despite my name, I am a type of jellyfish shaped like a plastic bag. My long tentacles float on top of the water, and a big sting from them can make someone very sick. If it is untreated, it can even kill.

4. I am found in Australia. I like to spin webs in hidden spots, so you may find me among rocks or wood piles, or in sheds. This means that humans often disturb me by mistake, and sometimes I will bite.

5. I am brown, with a long narrow body. I slither across the ground and hide in burrows or piles of leaves. If I feel threatened, I attack with poisonous fangs, and if medicine is not given quickly, my bite can be fatal. Beware!

ROOKIE
true or false?
Scorpions are closely related to spiders.

GENIUS
true or false?
there are no venomous mammals in the world.

STRENGTH IN NUMBERS

If you think sharing a bedroom with your sibling is a squeeze, think again! Many animals live in huge groups, and some insect colonies contain millions of inhabitants. Let's find out how much you know about them...

NEWBIE

1. A beehive can be packed with as many as 60,000 honeybees during the height of summer. How much honey will each worker bee produce in its lifetime?

A) $1/12$ a teaspoon
B) 5 teaspoons
C) a cup

2. In Antarctica, thousands of emperor penguins group together on the ice, in temperatures as low as –58°F (–50°C). But why do they huddle?

A) so they don't get lost in the blizzards
B) to protect them from predators
C) to stay warm

3. The largest known bat colony in the world at Bracken Cave, Texas, has up to 20 million bats roosting there. Each night the colony eats 140 tons of insects, which is about the same weight as:

A) an adult blue whale
B) a school bus
C) you and your classmates

4. So many flamingos flock to Lake Bogoria in Kenya that the shores look pink, but why are these birds' feathers pink?

A) Predators can't see the color pink.
B) The heat of the sun fades their feathers from red to pink.
C) Chemicals in the shrimp and algae they eat make them pink.

5. Termites build huge nests underground, with large chimney-like mounds aboveground. The tallest mound was found in Democratic Republic of Congo. How tall was it?

A) 42 feet (12.8 m) tall, about the same height as seven men
B) 19 feet (5.8 m) tall, about the same height as three men
C) 5.9 feet (1.8 m) tall, about the same height as one man

ROOKIE

1. How do worker bees tell the rest of their colony that they have found a good source of nectar?

A) they click their antennae together to tap out directions in a code.
B) they do a special dance, waggling their rear ends to show the other workers which direction to fly in.
C) they gather a group of bees at the entrance to the hive and lead them back to the flowers.

2. Army ants live life on the move. But how does the colony shelter when they stop for a while?

A) they find a hollow space, such as a hole in a tree trunk, and make a nest.
B) the worker ants link their legs together to make a "living nest" around the queen, so she is protected.
C) A group of worker ants goes on ahead, building anthills for the rest of the colony.

3. Locusts are dreaded by farmers, as a swarm can strip a whole field bare. But how long would it take them to do this?

A) a few hours
B) a couple of days
C) a couple of weeks

GENIUS

true or false?
The largest ant colony in the world stretches for around 62 miles (100km).

MIND-BOGGLING MIGRATION

Some animals don't just live in big groups, they travel for miles together during the migration season. But how much do you know about these epic journeys?

Can you match each of these animals with the right migration story?

A) CARIBOU

B) GEESE

C) CHRISTMAS ISLAND RED CRABS

D) SALMON

E) WILDEBEEST

1. Unusually, we live on land. But when we breed, we go back to the coast on our island. With millions of us scuttling along slowly, roads are closed so we can travel safely!

2. We are found in Canada and America. In fall, we begin our migration, flying huge distances in a "V" formation. Sometimes our journey takes us as far as Northern Europe.

3. We swim for miles upriver, battling strong currents and rapids to our spawning grounds. Sometimes you can see us leaping from the water as we tackle waterfalls and other obstacles in our way.

4. My herd lives in Northern Canada. Every year, we migrate north during the spring and travel back south in the fall. In a year, we can cover more than 3,728 miles (6,000km).

5. We live in Africa. From July to October, we make the journey from the Serengeti in Tanzania to the Masai Mara in Kenya. Over two million of us travel in a huge thundering herd. We must watch out for the hungry lions and crocodiles waiting to eat us for lunch!

NEWBIE

NEWBIE

ROOKIE

True or false?

When monarch butterflies migrate from Canada to Mexico, it's such a long way that no single butterfly survives the distance. Females lay eggs and their children continue the epic journey.

GENIUS

How far does the Arctic tern fly in a year?

A) 13,670 miles (22,000km) – halfway around the world

B) 28,583 miles (46,000km) – just over once around the world

C) 43,496 miles (70,000km) – almost twice around the world

YOU SCRATCH MY BACK...

Have you ever done a favor for a friend? Well, believe it or not, life's no different in the natural world, where some very odd animal combos are found lending each other a hand...

NEWBIE

Can you find the right answer to each of these questions?

1. Why do sharks allow cleaner fish to eat their dead skin and parasites?

A) it keeps the sharks healthy
B) so they can try to eat them
C) they are so small the sharks don't notice them

2. Brown algae grows on the back of the spider crab. How does it help them?

A) it disguises them so they can't be seen on the seabed
B) the algae attracts sea creatures that the crab eats
C) it strengthens the crab's shell

3. The plover bird is really brave – it flies into the open mouth of a crocodile. Why doesn't it get eaten?

A) plovers are poisonous to crocodiles
B) the bird pecks meat from between the crocodile's teeth, keeping them clean and healthy
C) crocodiles cannot digest plovers, so they don't eat them

4. Oxpeckers are birds that help zebras by eating ticks from their skin. How else do they help?

A) zebras eat their droppings to stay healthy
B) they use their beaks to comb through the zebra's mane
C) if they are startled and fly off, it lets the herd know danger may be near

5 Bees fly from flower to flower, collecting nectar to make food. How does this help plants?

A) they carry pollen from one plant to another, which helps more plants to grow
B) it helps the plants grow more flowers
C) it helps the plants grow bigger

ROOKIE

true or false?

Humans don't have this sort of helpful relationship with animals.

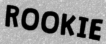

GENIUS

What is the name of an animal that lives on or in another animal, which causes it harm? Is it:

A) a host
B) bacteria
C) a parasite

INTO THE DEEP

We've explored the weird and wonderful world of animals, but now it's time to take a deep breath and dive into the mysterious world of the oceans. Are you ready to take the plunge?

SAILING THE SEVEN SEAS

All aboard! Let's set sail on the seven seas and see how much you know about our incredible oceans...

NEWBIE

True or False?

In the early to mid-1800s, if the seas were calm, the journey from Britain to Australia could take up to two months.

ROOKIE

1. The Southern Ocean surrounding Antarctica is one of the most remote places in the world. Sailors there face icebergs, rough seas, and freezing weather. No wonder it's called:

A) the "screaming seas"
B) the "frozen seas"
C) the "slow seas"

2. When ships had to rely on sails rather than engines, a crew would dread getting stuck in areas of calm weather, as it meant they could drift for days without a single puff of wind. This is known as the:

A) gale route
B) doldrums
C) swift seas

3. In the 18th century, Blackbeard was a terrible pirate who ruled the seas. He scared his victims by putting what in his beard?

A) slow-burning cannon fuses
B) mice
C) moldy food

4. In 1992, some containers fell off a ship traveling across the Pacific Ocean, spilling thousands of things into the sea. Since then, they have been tracked as they bob around the world. But what are they?

A) thousands of cell phones
B) thousands of rubber ducks
C) thousands of pairs of sneakers

5. How did ancient sailors find their way across oceans without a compass? Did they:

A) use the sun and stars to help them navigate
B) follow seabirds
C) just hope they were going in the right direction

GENIUS

True or False?

Canada's coastline is so long that it would take someone over six and a half months to drive all the way around it.

REEFS

Coral reefs are found in tropical waters. These amazing places have grown over thousands of years and teem with colorful fish and other ocean wildlife. How much do you know about them?

Can you match these coral reef questions with the right answers?

NEWBIE

1. What are coral reefs made from?

2. The Great Barrier Reef in Australia is the largest in the world. It stretches for 1,429 miles (2,300km), which is about the same distance by plane as...?

3. Which animals would you NOT find on a coral reef?

4. Which animals are coral related to?

5. What is needed for a coral reef to form?

A) penguins and polar bears

B) London, UK, to Athens, Greece

C) shallow, clear water that's warm and lots of sunlight

D) the remains of tiny animals called coral polyps

E) jellyfish and anemones

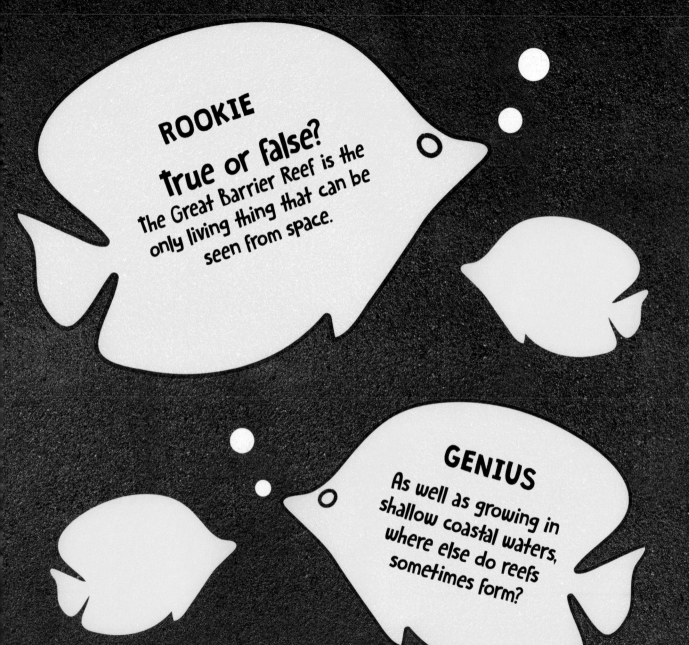

ROOKIE

True or false?
The Great Barrier Reef is the only living thing that can be seen from space.

GENIUS

As well as growing in shallow coastal waters, where else do reefs sometimes form?

65

DIVING DOWN

If you think your local swimming pool is deep, think again! Dive into the deepest water in the world, and it can take hours to reach the bottom, and you need more than a wetsuit to do it! How much do you know about the deep?

NEWBIE

Can you unscramble the words to find out more?

1. The deepest part of Earth's oceans is the RIAMANA trench.
2. It is found in the APFICIC Ocean.
3. The bottom of the trench is 35,814 feet (10,916 TRESEM) below the surface.
4. This is known as Challenger DPEE.
5. Scientists were surprised to find CERAUREST living there – they had thought that nothing could survive in water that deep.

Which of these three creatures is not found in the dark depths of the ocean?

1) I have ferocious-looking teeth, which give me my name: the fangtooth. I suck prey into my mouth, and, thanks to my terrible fangs, there's no escape!

2) I am a clownfish, and I have bright orange and white stripes. I like to live in sea anemones.

3) I am an angler fish. I have an enormous gaping mouth and what looks like a fishing line dangling in front of my terrible teeth. When hungry fish swim too close, I snap them up!

GENIUS

True or false?
The pressure of the water at the deepest point in the ocean is enough to crush bones.

OCEAN GIANTS

Lurking in the deep are some truly huge creatures, from killer whales to the giant squid, along with the ginormous blue whale. Let's find out more...

NEWBIE

See if you can find these ocean giants lurking in the word search.

B	L	U	E	W	H	A	L	E	N	T	P	F	E	T	M
K	R	C	G	W	D	G	R	S	T	G	K	H	S	I	N
I	S	R	I	H	S	I	F	Y	L	L	E	J	S	G	R
L	E	B	A	A	Y	A	N	A	R	K	G	N	O	E	K
L	T	F	I	L	R	N	I	O	G	E	N	T	I	E	R
E	I	S	O	E	F	T	M	I	A	S	A	A	L	P	A
R	R	O	A	S	L	S	B	T	C	S	R	A	R	Y	H
W	A	N	C	H	H	Q	K	E	B	C	H	I	O	A	S
H	O	S	Q	A	H	U	O	C	R	W	L	Y	C	R	G
A	B	R	N	R	S	I	I	E	N	T	P	N	O	A	N
L	B	E	R	K	I	D	R	I	K	N	E	G	D	T	I
E	I	N	C	V	F	D	F	P	O	A	H	A	I	N	K
M	R	I	B	O	R	P	A	P	P	L	P	N	L	A	S
G	S	S	E	L	A	H	W	M	R	E	P	S	E	M	A
G	I	A	N	T	O	C	T	O	P	U	S	T	U	H	B

blue whale
killer whale
giant squid
whale shark
fin whale
jellyfish
manta ray
sperm whale
oarfish
basking shark
giant octopus

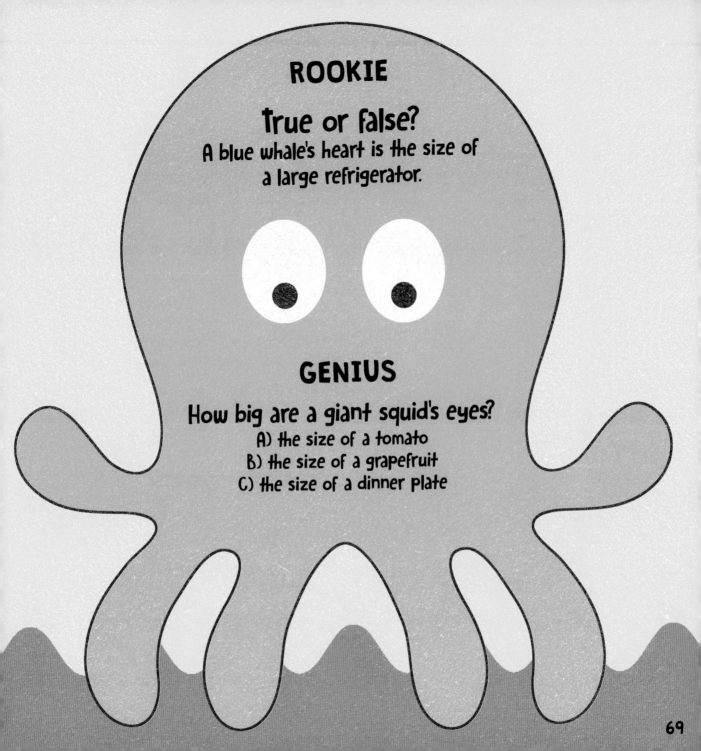

ROOKIE

True or false?
A blue whale's heart is the size of a large refrigerator.

GENIUS

How big are a giant squid's eyes?
A) the size of a tomato
B) the size of a grapefruit
C) the size of a dinner plate

DANGER IN THE DEEP

Ask people what scary animals live in the oceans and usually they will answer "sharks." But they're not the only creatures to be wary of if you go for a dip in the sea...

NEWBIE

Can you match the sea creatures with their deadly weapon?

1. Blue-ringed octopus

2. Tiger shark

3. Lionfish

4. Great white shark

5. Stingray

A) I have more than 300 razor-sharp teeth arranged in deadly rows and an extremely powerful bite. I am one of the most feared ocean creatures.

B) I am very pretty to look at, but don't be fooled. Hiding in long wavy fins on my back are venomous spines. One spike from me, and you will be in agony for hours!

C) I have terrible teeth, but they're not only in my mouth. My skin is made of toothlike structures, which feel smooth one way - but if prey brushes me the wrong way, they will be shredded!

D) I have a whiplike tail with stinging spines. It is powerful enough to pierce a human's chest.

E) I'm quite small, but don't let my size fool you. When I'm about to bite, bright blue circles appear all over my body. Strangely, my bite is completely painless. Many people don't know they've been bitten until it is too late...

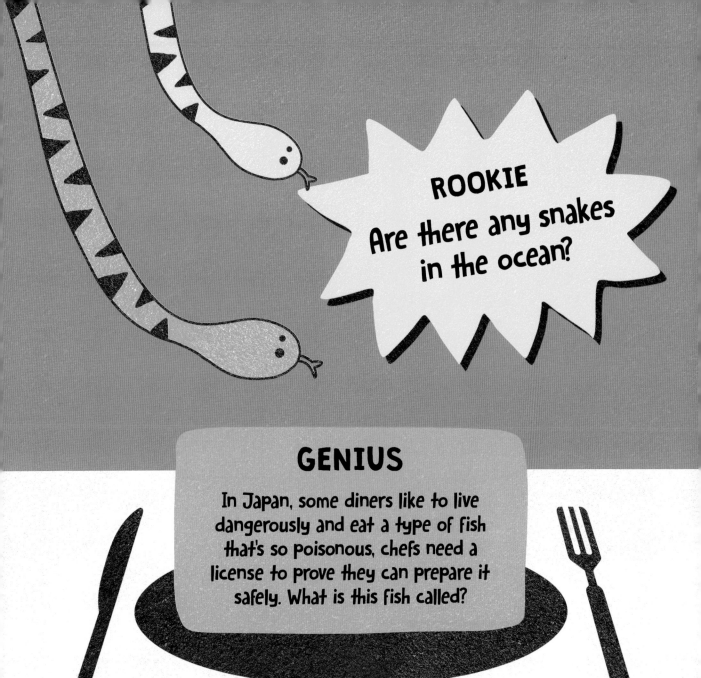

ROOKIE
Are there any snakes
in the ocean?

GENIUS

In Japan, some diners like to live dangerously and eat a type of fish that's so poisonous, chefs need a license to prove they can prepare it safely. What is this fish called?

INCREDIBLE PLACES

There are so many incredible places in our oceans. But how much do you know about them?

NEWBIE

Unscramble the words to find cool facts about some amazing underwater places:

1. The Denmark Strait Cataract is the tallest underwater ATALLERFW in the world.

2. The beach on Sanibel Island in Florida, USA, is made of SHSLLESAE!

3. The Blue RTGOTO in Anacapria, Italy, has water so blue it looks like a swimming pool!

4. Ha Long Bay in Vietnam is full of towering limestone PLALISR and islands.

5. Miami Beach in Florida, USA, is one of the world's most famous SNDARBAS.

True or false?
The Great Blue Hole, a large sinkhole off the coast of Belize, is over 328 feet (100 m) across and 79 feet (24 m) deep.

The Mokstraumen is found in the Norwegian Sea. But what is it?

A) a tidal whirlpool
B) a series of mysterious underwater caves
C) a coral reef

RIDE THE WAVES

Forget about gentle waves lapping the shore at the beach, these are monster waves! Are you brave enough to take them on?

NEWBIE

Can you find these wave words in the search?

A	L	R	E	B	R	A	L	E	O	P	P	F	O	A	M
K	R	C	G	W	R	G	R	S	L	L	E	W	S	I	N
I	S	R	I	H	S	E	F	Y	L	W	E	J	S	G	R
L	E	B	A	A	Y	A	A	A	R	K	G	N	O	E	K
M	T	T	I	D	E	N	I	K	G	E	N	T	I	E	R
E	I	S	O	E	F	T	M	I	E	S	A	A	L	P	H
R	R	O	A	S	L	S	B	T	C	R	R	A	W	Y	H
K	A	N	C	R	E	S	T	E	B	C	S	I	O	A	S
H	O	S	Q	A	H	U	O	C	R	W	L	Y	T	R	F
A	B	R	N	R	S	U	R	F	N	T	P	N	R	A	N
L	B	E	R	K	I	D	R	I	K	N	E	G	E	T	I
E	T	S	U	N	A	M	I	P	O	A	H	A	D	N	L
M	R	I	B	O	R	P	A	P	P	L	P	N	N	A	S
G	S	S	E	R	E	L	L	O	R	E	P	S	U	M	A
G	I	M	N	T	O	C	B	O	P	R	S	T	U	H	B

breakers
tsunami
surf
tide
crest
swell
undertow
foam
roller

74

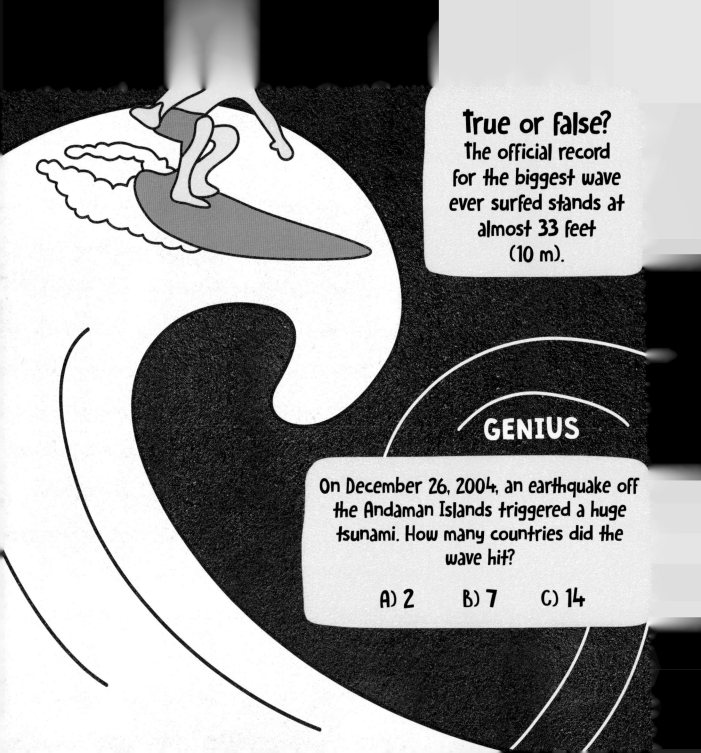

ISLANDS AND ATOLLS

The world's oceans are full of islands – from tiny specks of land to sweeping tropical paradises. How much island info do you know?

NEWBIE

Which of these two islands is larger: Greenland or Madagascar?

ROOKIE

True or false?

1. In 1963, volcanic eruptions created a new island called Surtsey, near Iceland.
2. There are 30,000 islands in the Pacific Ocean.
3. It takes three days to reach Tristan da Cunha, one of the world's most remote islands, which is in the South Atlantic Ocean.
4. In 2009, a meeting was held at the bottom of the ocean in the Maldives, to highlight the risk of them completely flooding because of global warming.
5. Japan is made up of 100 islands.

GENIUS

Alcatraz Island, off San Francisco, is famous because:

A) it's where the explorer Christopher Columbus landed
B) it's the home of the Statue of Liberty
C) it has a prison that no one ever successfully escaped from

AMAZING JOURNEYS

Some of these animals travel enormous distances every year, but can you identify the travelers from the ones that stay put?

NEWBIE

Choose the six animals that migrate from the list below:

humpback whale	sea urchin
hermit crab	sardine
stonefish	starfish
Adélie penguin	limpet
hagfish	sea anemone
sea cucumber	gray whale
elephant seal	tuna

Female leatherback turtles migrate back
to the beaches where they hatched.
Why do they do this?

A) to lay eggs
B) to die
C) to visit their parents

GENIUS

What are drift seeds?

A) seeds that are carried by seabirds
B) seeds that are dispersed by the ocean
C) seeds that are carried by the wind

WHEN DISASTER STRIKES

Extreme events happen all over the planet – from earth-shattering earthquakes to vicious volcanoes. Is your knowledge of them red-hot, or is it a total disaster? Let's find out!

NEWBIE

Severe storms with high winds have three different names, depending on which part of the world they hit. They are called:

A) cyclones, hurricanes, and typhoons
B) cloudbursts, downpours, and washouts

WILD WEATHER

Hurricanes and tornadoes are responsible for some really wild weather. Let's see if you can storm through these questions...

ROOKIE

true or false?
The highest wind speeds ever recorded for a hurricane were the same speed as:

A) a midsize car driven at full speed
B) a Formula 1 racing car
C) a 747 jumbo jet

Here are six descriptions of wild weather. Three describe hurricanes and the others, tornadoes. Can you figure out which is which?

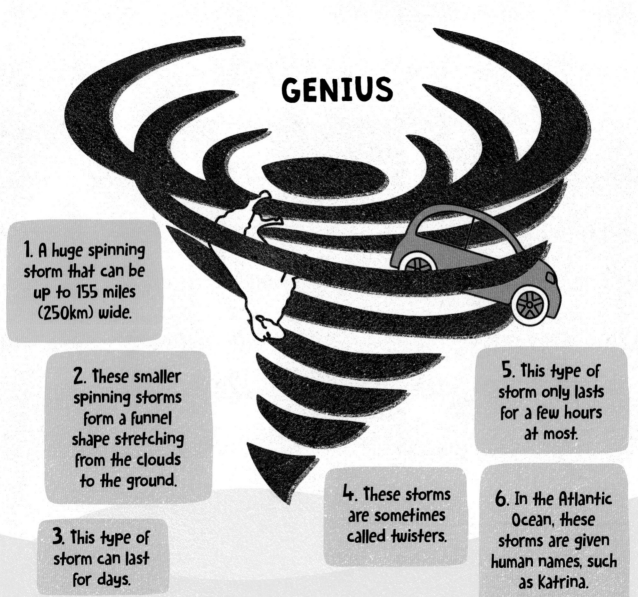

GENIUS

1. A huge spinning storm that can be up to 155 miles (250km) wide.

2. These smaller spinning storms form a funnel shape stretching from the clouds to the ground.

3. This type of storm can last for days.

4. These storms are sometimes called twisters.

5. This type of storm only lasts for a few hours at most.

6. In the Atlantic Ocean, these storms are given human names, such as Katrina.

SCARY STORMS

From rumbling thunder to electrifying lightning, is your know-how absolutely awful or blindingly brilliant? There's only one way to find out...

NEWBIE

1. How hot is a bolt of lightning?

A) hotter than an exploding volcano
B) hotter than the highest setting on a stove
C) hotter than the surface of the sun

2. How can you tell how far away a thunderstorm is?

A) When there is a gap of more than 30 seconds between the thunder and lightning, it is right over you.
B) Count the number of seconds between lightning and thunder. If there's a gap of a second, the storm is about a quarter of a mile (a third of a kilometer) away.
C) If there is forked lightning, the storm is directly overhead.

3. How big is the largest hailstone ever recorded?

A) the size of a ping-pong ball
B) the size of a tennis ball
C) the size of a small soccer ball

4. What is the most number of times a person has been struck by lightning and survived?

A) seven times
B) three times
C) once

5. Which of these places is safest in a thunderstorm?

A) a golf course
B) inside a car
C) under a tree

ROOKIE
True or false?
In Venezuela, the Catatumbo lightning produces half a million lightning strikes a year.

GENIUS

Blizzards are snowstorms that come with bitingly cold temperatures and dump massive amounts of snow in a matter of hours. But which of these places in the USA holds the record for the most snowfall?

A) Valdez, Alaska
B) Glacier National Park, Montana
C) Tamarack, California

HORRIBLE HEATWAVES

Let's find out how much you know about horrible heatwaves.
Is your knowledge scorching hot or lukewarm?

S	P	A	G	L	E	P	H	S	N	T	P	F	E	T	M
I	R	C	G	A	S	U	N	S	T	G	K	H	S	I	N
A	G	R	I	U	Z	I	Y	N	E	A	R	U	T	O	H
R	P	B	A	R	Y	K	N	A	R	K	G	N	O	E	P
C	A	L	S	C	O	R	C	H	E	D	N	T	I	R	O
N	R	S	U	O	F	Y	M	I	A	S	A	A	C	P	B
G	C	E	M	E	W	W	I	T	E	S	F	A	R	S	H
E	H	N	M	D	H	T	K	E	B	C	Y	I	G	R	F
K	E	B	E	U	I	T	P	C	A	I	L	Y	C	I	B
E	D	R	R	H	D	L	I	E	K	T	P	N	R	R	O
D	B	E	R	O	E	I	R	O	I	N	E	G	D	D	C
V	I	N	C	V	A	D	K	P	N	A	H	A	I	O	G
M	R	I	B	O	D	P	A	P	G	L	P	N	L	N	N
G	S	T	H	G	U	O	R	D	T	T	U	A	E	M	I
C	E	S	N	A	I	D	N	H	I	A	D	T	U	H	K

Find these
heatwave
words in the
grid above:

sun
baking
drought
dry

scorched
summer
parched
hot

Can you survive a heatwave? Read the tips below and figure out which ones will help you keep cool, and which would make you a dangerous fool!

1. Make sure you wear dark clothes.

2. Drink plenty of water.

3. Lie out in the sun, whatever the temperature.

4. Make sure you wear a thick coat and woolly hat.

5. Wear cool, loose clothing.

6. Go out for a long run.

7. Stay indoors at the hottest time of the day.

8. Don't leave your dog in the car.

9. Make sure your pets stay cool.

10. Diving head first into a river or lake.

GENIUS

How many years did the longest drought in California last?

A) 10 years
B) 22 years
C) 78 years
D) 240 years

TERRIBLE EARTHQUAKES

Earthquakes may be just a little wobble, or they can be strong enough to bring down buildings and bridges, buckle train tracks, and rip up roads. Check out these earth-shaking questions and see how you score...

NEWBIE

Can you figure out which of these tips will help you in an earthquake and which are just plain silly?

1. If you live in an earthquake zone, make sure you have an emergency kit containing food, clothing, a first aid kit, and a portable radio.

2. If you are out driving, stop and take shelter under a bridge.

3. As soon as the earthquake starts, drop to the floor.

4. Curl up under heavy furniture such as a table and hold on.

5. Stand under a doorframe.

ROOKIE

How long ago was the first earthquake detector invented?

A) 2,000 years ago   C) 140 years ago
B) 300 years ago   D) 46 years ago

GENIUS

True or false?

Most of the world's earthquakes happen within a ring around the Atlantic Ocean.

FIERY VOLCANOES

They're extremely explosive, unpredictable, and very scary. No, not your teacher – we're talking about volcanoes! Can you take the heat?

NEWBIE

Can you figure out the volcano words in the list below?

mountain

shells

cone

lava

sand

eruption

shore

ash

tide

smoke

waves

seaweed

For a bonus point, group together the other words in the list. What sort of place do they describe?

ROOKIE

The loudest volcanic eruption ever was Krakatoa, in Indonesia, which exploded in 1883, destroying most of the island. How far away was the explosion heard?

A) Malaysia – 746 miles (1,200km) away
B) Vietnam – 1,429 miles (2,300km) away
C) The Philippines – 1,740 miles (2,800km) away
D) Australia – 2,299 miles (3,700km) away

GENIUS

Match the names of the volcanoes with the right description:

1. In 1902, this mountain erupted, destroying the port city of St. Pierre.
2. Probably the most famous volcanic eruption, which happened in Europe in AD 79, covering the town of Pompeii in ash.
3. The ash cloud from this volcano's eruption in 2010 disrupted air travel for several weeks all the way across the Atlantic Ocean.
4. In 1980, this volcano exploded so violently that an entire side of the mountain was blown away.
5. This volcano was born in 1943, suddenly erupting in the middle of a farmer's field. In just over a year, the cone stood at more than 1,083 feet (330 m) tall!

A) Mount Vesuvius, Italy
B) Mount St. Helens, USA
C) Mont Pelée, Martinique

D) Paricutin, Mexico
E) Eyjafjallajokull, Iceland

Floods can be a nightmare, but how much do you know about them? Is your brain awash with facts or do you need rescuing?

NEWBIE

Unscramble these flood words to find out more:

1. The worst floods in world history happened in GNIHA in 1931, when an area almost the size of Britain was flooded.
2. ASLFH floods can sweep away everything in their path – even cars and bridges!
3. The Thames Barrier is the world's largest movable flood barrier, which protects DONNOL from flooding.
4. Even ESTRESD can have floods!
5. A fast-flowing flood can knock down a SEORNP even if they're just 1 foot (30 cm) deep!

ROOKIE

Which European country reclaims land from the sea, which means it needs huge flood defenses?
A) France
B) the Netherlands
C) Switzerland

GENIUS

true or false?

the largest flood in the world, 25,000 years ago, was so powerful that boulders were carried from Montana, in the Midwest of the USA, all the way to Vancouver, on the west coast of Canada.

TERRIFYING TSUNAMIS

Earthquakes are bad enough, but when the ground stops shaking, danger lurks near the sea in the form of walls of water called tsunamis. Can you handle these questions, or will you be overwhelmed?

NEWBIE

The Indian Ocean tsunami that hit on December 26, 2004, was one of the biggest disasters in modern history. See if you can answer these true or false questions about it:

1) The earthquake that caused the tsunami was so powerful that it is known as a "megathrust earthquake."

2) Only six earthquakes of this size have been recorded since the early 1900s.

3) Before the tsunami hit, the sea moved away from the shore by up to 1.5 miles (2.5km).

4) A 10-year-old girl who was vacationing in Thailand warned other vacationers that the tsunami was coming, having learned about tsunamis at school and saving hundreds of people.

5) The earthquake that caused the tsunami was so powerful it shortened the day slightly.

In 1958 an earthquake in Lituya Bay, Alaska, caused a tsunami with waves so tall they reached about the same height as:

A) the London Eye, London
B) the Eiffel Tower, Paris
C) the Great Pyramid of Giza, Egypt
D) One World Trade Center, New York

GENIUS

The Japan earthquake of 2010 moved its main island, Honshu, east by how much:

A) 0.001 inches (0.2mm)
B) 0.08 inches (2mm)
C) 0.8 inches (2cm)
D) 7 feet (2m)

SLIPPERY AVALANCHES AND MUDSLIDES

Can you imagine being swept away in a wall of icy snow or a river of oozing mud? How much do you know about avalanches and mudslides? Let's find out!

NEWBIE

Can you find these avalanche words in the grid below?

B	L	E	B	W	H	L	W	E	T	S	A	F	E	T	M
K	R	C	G	W	D	G	R	S	T	G	K	H	S	I	N
I	S	R	I	A	V	A	L	A	N	C	H	E	S	G	R
L	S	B	A	A	Y	A	N	A	R	K	G	N	O	E	B
L	E	L	I	L	R	S	L	O	P	E	N	T	I	E	E
E	A	S	I	E	F	T	M	I	S	S	A	A	L	P	A
G	R	O	A	D	L	S	B	T	N	S	R	A	R	Y	C
W	C	N	C	H	E	Q	K	E	I	C	H	I	C	E	O
H	H	S	Q	A	H	U	O	C	A	W	L	Y	C	R	N
O	B	R	N	R	S	I	I	E	T	T	P	N	O	A	N
L	B	E	R	K	N	D	R	I	N	N	E	G	D	T	I
E	I	N	C	V	O	D	F	P	U	A	H	A	I	N	K
M	R	I	B	O	W	P	A	P	O	L	P	N	L	A	S
G	S	S	E	L	A	H	W	M	M	E	P	S	E	M	A
G	I	E	U	C	S	E	R	O	P	U	P	T	U	H	B

AVALANCHE
SNOW
ICE
MOUNTAIN
SLIDE
FAST
SEARCH
RESCUE
BEACON
SLOPE

ROOKIE

In 1999, an avalanche hit Galtur in Austria. How long did it take for it to travel down the mountain?

A) 2 minutes
B) 10 minutes
C) less than a minute
D) 5 minutes

GENIUS

Are avalanches powerful enough to destroy a whole village?

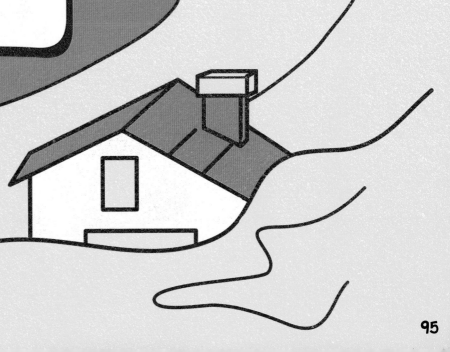

BLAZING WILDFIRES

When a wildfire starts, you'd better stay far away. The fierce flames will devour everything in their path. So let's see how you fare — are you on fire, or has your know-how fizzled out?

NEWBIE

Which of these things may start a wildfire?

volcanoes erupting

lightning

sparks from rock falls

spontaneous combustion

discarded cigarettes

machinery sparks

smoldering campfires

downed powerlines

ROOKIE

How fast did the flames from Australia's Black Saturday bushfires travel?

A) 2mph (4kph) – about the pace of a snail
B) 1mph (1.6kph) – about the pace of a millipede
C) 3.75mph (6kph) – the pace of a human walking
D) 7.5mph (12kph) – about the pace of a human running

GENIUS

True or false?
Bushfires can help some plants to grow.

EXTREME PLACES

You have to be tough to survive in some of Earth's most extreme places. Let's see whether you have what it takes, or if you're better off staying at home...

THE ARCTIC

It's tough at the top of the world. Can you crack these questions on the icy Arctic, or will you slip up? Let's find out!

NEWBIE

In all these Arctic lists, there's an odd one out. Can you spot each one?

1) Animals: polar bear, harp seal, narwhal, kangaroo, Arctic tern, Arctic fox

2) Features: ice sheet, tundra, iceberg, outback, crevasse, glacier

3) Weather: blizzard, whiteout, heatwave, snow, frost, freezing

4) Clothing: thermal underwear, waterproof boots, bathing suit, snow goggles, fleece gloves

5) Places: North Pole, Arctic Ocean, Arctic Circle, Sydney, Laptev Sea, Barents Sea

Bonus question
Each of the odd ones out on the list above gives you a clue.

Put them together to see if you can guess which country they belong to.

ROOKIE

Who was the first person to reach the North Pole?

A) Robert Peary
B) Frederick Cook
C) no one knows for sure if it was Peary or Cook

GENIUS

What is the biggest danger in the Arctic?

THE ANTARCTIC

The Arctic may be tough, but Antarctica is totally harsh, just like some of these questions! Can you rise to the challenge or will you freeze completely?

NEWBIE

Facts or fibs? Can you figure out which are which?

1) In Antarctica, winter is from June to August every year.

2) A satellite recently recorded a new low temperature of –138.5°F (–94.7°C).

3) In summer, the ice in Antarctica melts completely.

4) The biggest danger in Antarctica is polar bears.

5) The largest land animal in Antartica is a tiny insect.

6) No one has ever reached the South Pole.

7) In winter, it stays light for weeks at a time.

8) Some icebergs floating near Antarctica are blue.

ROOKIE

Unscramble the word to see how scientists cope with the cold:

In Antarctica, when scientists are working outside, they breathe using a NOELKRS inside their coat, so the air is warmed a little bit before it reaches their lungs.

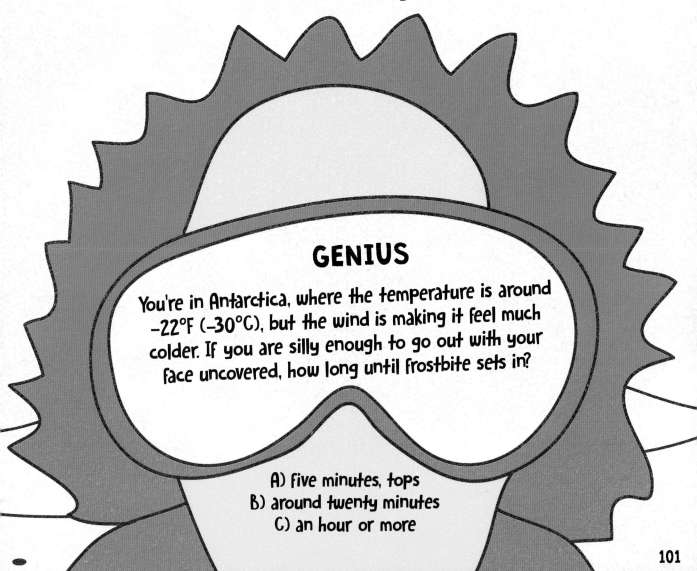

GENIUS

You're in Antarctica, where the temperature is around -22°F (-30°C), but the wind is making it feel much colder. If you are silly enough to go out with your face uncovered, how long until frostbite sets in?

A) five minutes, tops
B) around twenty minutes
C) an hour or more

MOST DANGEROUS ROADS

Warning! Hazards ahead! If you choose to take one of these road trips, you are taking your life in your hands. Let's see if you have the dangers sussed.

NEWBIE

1. If you take Italy's Stelvio Pass, how many hair-raising hairpin bends will you have to drive around?

A) 2
B) 8
C) 17
D) 48

2. Bolivia's El Camino de la Muerte is just 10 feet (3 m) wide, with no guardrails to stop vehicles plummeting 1,970 feet (600 m) in places. No wonder its name means:

A) the narrow road
B) the hell road
C) the death road
D) the fool's road

3. The Trans-Sahara Highway is truly scary. Searing 122°F (50°C) heat, no rest areas. What do you need to drive this road?

A) experience in desert driving
B) your own fuel, water, and food
C) know-how to fix your car if it breaks down
D) a 4 x 4 vehicle
E) all of the above

4. What is one of the biggest problems when you reach the Costa Rica section of the Pan-American Highway?

A) the road is often washed away
B) the heat melts tires
C) heavy rainfall makes driving difficult
D) rainforest trees falling across the road
E) all of the above

5. The Dalton Highway in Alaska is so remote it boasts the longest stretch of road without any rest areas – no fuel, toilets, or food. But just how far between rest areas is it?

A) 240 miles (386km)
B) 67 miles (108km)
C) 175 miles (282km)
D) 132 miles (213km)

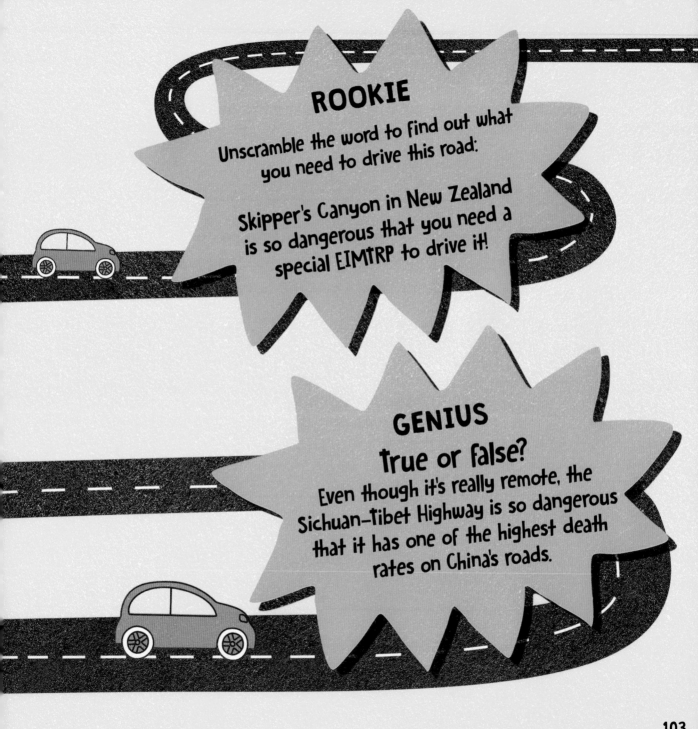

ROOKIE

Unscramble the word to find out what you need to drive this road:

Skipper's Canyon in New Zealand is so dangerous that you need a special EIMtRP to drive it!

GENIUS

True or false?

Even though it's really remote, the Sichuan-Tibet Highway is so dangerous that it has one of the highest death rates on China's roads.

DRIEST PLACES

The world's driest places are also some of the toughest. How much do you know about them? Are you swimming in knowledge, or has your brainpower dried up? Let's see...

NEWBIE

The driest place on Earth is the Atacama Desert in Chile. Below you can read several statements. Can you figure out which are facts and which are fakes?

1) In some parts of the Atacama Desert, rainfall has never been recorded.
2) In 2001, there were flash floods in the region.
3) In some places it's so dry that nothing decomposes, so dead vegetation may be thousands of years old!
4) Many farmers grow their crops in the desert.
5) Few plants and animals are able to survive in the Atacama.

Can you match each creature listed below with its desert survival superpower?

1. desert tortoise

2. sand grouse

3. thorny devil

4. fogstand beetle

5. camel

A) These animals, often called "ships of the desert," can drink up to 12 gallons (46 liters) of water at a time before lasting several weeks without.

B) This lizard soaks up dew through its skin.

C) This bird can carry water in its feathers.

D) Adults can go for up to a year without drinking water, getting it from food instead.

E) This creature stands still and lets the morning fog condense on its body, which it then drinks.

GENIUS

The giant saguaro cactus grows to an incredible 49 feet (15 m) tall – more than the height of eight people standing on each other's shoulders! But how much water can it hold?

A) enough to fill 12 bathtubs
B) enough to fill 75 bathtubs
C) it doesn't store any water

HIGHEST PLACES IN THE WORLD

Living at a high altitude can be tricky. There's less oxygen, which can make your brain feel fuzzy. Can you hit the heights or will you get stuck at rock bottom? Let's find out.

NEWBIE

Can you find some of the world's highest places in the word search?

A	L	R	E	B	R	A	L	E	O	P	P	F	O	A	M
X	R	C	I	M	O	K	R	S	L	L	H	A	S	A	N
I	S	R	I	H	S	E	F	Y	L	L	E	J	S	G	S
L	E	E	A	A	Y	A	O	R	U	R	O	N	O	E	H
L	T	L	I	D	E	N	I	K	G	E	N	T	I	E	I
I	I	A	O	E	F	T	P	O	T	O	S	I	L	P	G
R	R	L	A	S	L	J	B	T	C	R	R	A	W	Y	A
J	A	T	C	R	E	S	U	E	B	C	S	I	O	A	T
H	O	O	Q	A	H	U	O	L	R	W	L	Y	T	R	S
A	B	R	N	R	S	U	R	F	I	T	P	N	R	A	E
L	B	E	R	L	A	P	A	Z	K	A	E	G	E	T	I
E	T	S	U	N	A	M	I	P	O	A	C	A	D	N	L
L	E	A	D	V	I	L	L	E	P	L	P	A	N	A	S
G	S	S	E	R	E	L	L	O	R	E	P	S	U	M	A
G	I	M	L	A	Y	A	B	O	P	R	S	T	U	H	B

LHASA (Tibet)

EL ALTO (Bolivia)

LA PAZ (Bolivia)

POTOSI (Bolivia)

SHIGATSE (Tibet)

JULIACA (Peru)

ORURU (Bolivia)

LAYA (Bhutan)

KOMIC (India)

LEADVILLE (USA)

ROOKIE

How do commuters travel between the city and the slopes of La Paz, Bolivia?

A) subway
B) bus
C) cable car

GENIUS

Because there is less oxygen, tourists who visit high altitudes may have problems, such as: difficulties eating, sleeping, and digesting food, feeling nauseous, headaches. How can they prevent them?

A) ascend slowly over several days so the body acclimatizes
B) ascend really quickly so that the body gets used to it really quickly
C) take medicine to help the body adjust

BONUS QUESTION

True or false?

In the gold mines of La Rinconada, Peru, the world's highest city, miners work for free for 30 days. On the 31st day, they carry away as much rock as they can – whatever gold they find is their payment.

MOST POLLUTED PLACES TO LIVE

Whether it's dirt, smog, chemicals, trash, or a combination of them all, pollution stinks. Let's see if you can clean up with your answers...

NEWBIE

Unscramble these words to find out how poisonous pollution can be.

1. In Norilsk, Russia, pollution is so bad that no RESET grow within 19 miles (30km) of the city.

2. In Linfen, China, it's said that thanks to pollution, UYLNARD hung out to dry turns black.

3. Even outer space can't escape — there are 500,000 pieces of space debris orbiting AHTRE.

4. Mexico City sits in a volcanic crater, which means pollution results in thick MOGS hanging over the city.

5. An explosion at a UCLEARN reactor in Chernobyl, Ukraine, means that the area has been unsafe for more than 30 years.

ROOKIE

True or false?
Light and noise are types of pollution.

GENIUS

Which continent is the least polluted on Earth?

MOST REMOTE SETTLEMENTS

Imagine living in a place so remote that even in the age of online shopping, supply ships only arrive a few times a year! See if you can seek out the truth about these remote places:

NEWBIE

Find the names of these remote islands in the grid.

```
A L R E B R A L E O P R Y O D M
K R C I M O K R S L L A A S A N
I E A S T E R F Y L L O J S G S
L E E A Y A U R U R U N O E H
E T L G I L B E R T E L T I E I
I B A O E F T P F T O S I C P G
R R E A S L J B A C R R A O Y A
A A T A R E S U R B E S I C A D
U O O Q R H U O O R G L Y O R L
Q B R N R S U R E I R P N S A I
C B E R L A P A S K O E G E T K
A T S U N A M I P O E C A D N T
M P I T C A I R N P G P A N A S
G S S E R E L L O R T P S U M A
G I M L S Y A B O P S S T U H B
```

EASTER
COCOS
FAROES
PITCAIRN
BEAR
St. KILDA
RAOUL
St. GEORGE
MACQUARIE
GILBERT

ROOKIE

True or false?

When a Swedish explorer crossed Chang Tang in the Tibetan Plateau, he didn't see a single person for more than 45 days.

GENIUS

Supai, Arizona, is very hard to reach as it's at the bottom of the Grand Canyon. There are no roads, so how is the mail brought in?

A) by mule

B) by helicopter

C) there is no mail service

D) on foot

MOST CROWDED PLACES TO LIVE

Supercharged city or people-packed town – some places on planet Earth are crammed with wall-to-wall people. Is your brain just as full of facts?

NEWBIE

Which is more crowded, New York City or Manila, in the Philippines?

ROOKIE Match the places with the number of people who live there.

1. Tokyo-Yakahama, Japan
2. London, United Kingdom
3. Sydney, Australia
4. Los Angeles, USA
5. Mumbai, India

A) 22.8 million
B) 4 million
C) 15.3 million
D) 10.3 million
E) 37.7 million

GENIUS

Santa Cruz del Islote, off the coast of Colombia, is a tiny island less than .007 square miles (0.012 sq km) in size. How many people live there?

A) 123
B) 291

C) 675
D) 1,200

WETTEST PLACES

From brief drizzle to sudden downpours, we've all been caught off guard by the rain. Can you keep calm and carry on, or will the rain suspend play? Let's find out!

True or false?
1. Scotland holds the UK record for the most consecutive days of rain, at 89.
2. The oldest fossilized raindrops found fell to Earth 2,000 years ago.
3. Raindrops can reach speeds of up to 3mph (5kph).
4. Red, yellow, and black rain has fallen in Kerala, India.
5. It's possible for scientists to make it rain.

NEWBIE

ROOKIE

Cherrapunji in India holds the record for the most rainfall in a year. But how much rain fell?

A) 85 feet (26 m) – almost the height of a nine-story building!
B) 15 feet (4.5 m) – around the same height as a double-decker bus!
C) 7 feet (2 m) – slightly more than the height of a man!

GENIUS

The distinct earthy aroma you can smell after rain falls is called:

A) petrified

B) putrefied

C) petrichor

PECULIAR PLACES

They often say that truth is stranger than fiction, and with these questions, that's spot-on. Get ready for a whirlwind tour of some of the world's quirkiest customs and wackiest facts:

Here are some most peculiar place names. Let's see if you know your Boring from your Normal by guessing which places are real and which are fake!

NEWBIE

1. Accident, a place in Maryland, USA
2. Batman, a city in Turkey
3. Boring, a town in Oregon, USA, twinned with a place called Dull in Scotland!
4. Bra, a small village in Italy
5. Catbrain, a village in Gloucestershire, UK
6. Earth, a town in Texas, USA
7. Eiderdown, a hamlet in Scotland
8. Flipchart, a village in Ireland
9. Gotham, pronounced "Goat-em," a small village in Nottinghamshire, UK
10. Normal, a town in Illinois, USA
11. Ribcage, a town in Alaska, USA
12. Skippingrope, an island in Western Australia
13. Soupspoon, a small town in Canada
14. Vulcan, a town in Alberta, Canada (popular with *Star Trek* fans!)
15. Wee Waa, a town in New South Wales, Australia

What hidden meanings do place names have?

A) they can describe the landscape
B) they can be named after people
C) the name can tell you who founded the place
D) they may be named after explorers

The longest place name in the world is New Zealand's: Taumatawhakatangi-hangakoauauotamatea-turipukakapikimaunga-horonukupokaiwhenuakitanatahu, with 85 letters. How many letters do the shortest place names have?

A) 4   B) 2   C) 1

Can you name one of the world's shortest place names?

MANNERS MATTER

Good manners can open doors, but it's worth remembering that what's polite in one country may be extremely rude in another. Do you have what it takes to charm people? Let's find out!

NEWBIE

Can you match the country with the polite way to behave?

1. Netherlands

2. Turkey

3. South Korea

4. Vietnam

5. Russia

6. Venezuela

A) In this country, you should always arrive 10 to 15 minutes late for a dinner invitation. Being on time is seen as being greedy!

B) In this country, always remove your shoes before entering someone's home.

C) If you give someone a bouquet of flowers, make sure it has an odd number of blossoms. Even numbers are only for graves.

D) You should always accept a gift with both hands.

E) In this country, you should wait for your elders to start their meal first.

F) Don't give knives or scissors as a gift here, as it's considered bad luck.

If you are dining out in China, how can you show your appreciation to your hosts?

A) by burping loudly
B) by giving them a round of applause
C) by washing the dishes

GENIUS

Is there anywhere in the world where chewing gum is illegal?

THE WHOLE TRUTH?

We all know stealing will get you arrested, and speeding will earn you a ticket, but there are plenty of laws that are just baffling. Are you ready to play judge and jury?

NEWBIE

Which of these laws are loopy but true and which are downright lies?

1. In London, England, men must not wear bowler hats on a Friday.
2. In Venice, Italy, it is against the law to travel by gondola.
3. In Vermont, USA, a woman needs the written permission of her husband to wear dentures.
4. In Russia, it is illegal to sing when there is snow on the ground.
5. In French swimming pools, men must wear swim briefs, not loose-fitting swim shorts.
6. In Germany, it's illegal to run out of fuel on the autobahn (highway).
7. It is illegal to hoist the national flag after 8 pm in Montreal, Canada.
8. It is illegal in France to name a pig Napoléon.
9. In Scotland, it is against the law for men to wear underwear with a kilt.
10. In Britain, it's treason to stick a postage stamp upside down on an envelope.

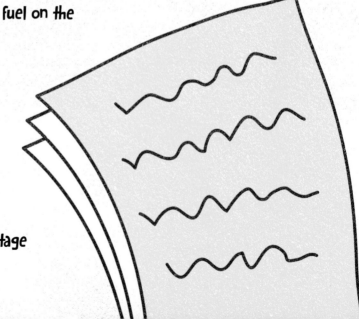

ROOKIE

Unscramble the anagram to find out about this crazy traffic law:

In Alabama, USA, it is illegal to drive while LIDLDEDOFNB.

GENIUS

True or false?

For a while in England during the 17th century, celebrating Christmas was banned.

WORLD'S STRANGEST JOBS

If you think school is tough, think again. Let's take a look at some of the world's strangest jobs and see if you can earn some points.

NEWBIE

Unscramble the words to find out what each of these real live workers do for a living:

1. This person spends all day tasting ETP OODF.

2. This person goes out to collect the fattest, juiciest OMSRW to sell to fishermen.

3. How about spending the day milking SENKAS for their venom?

4. If you are good with words, how about being a TNEUORF IEOKOC writer?

5. Ethical HAKESRC test companies' websites to see if they are secure.

ROOKIE

True or false?

Before there were electronic computers, some people had a job where they were known as "computers" and did huge complicated calculations by hand.

GENIUS

Which of these was NOT a job in the past:

A) Whipping boy – a stand-in who was punished instead of the prince

B) Tea caddy – a child employed to carry tea-making equipment for rich people

C) Nightsoil man – went around at night collecting... em... poop

D) Knocknobbler – employed to chase dogs from church

FABULOUS FESTIVALS

Festivals are held all over the world. Some are centuries old, while others are more modern creations. Is your brain packed with a fiesta full of festival facts? Time to find out.

NEWBIE

C	E	A	O	I	K	A	L	I	Y	Q	K	F	E	Z	M
I	R	C	G	A	S	G	E	S	T	G	J	H	S	I	D
A	I	A	H	A	A	G	J	I	A	N	G	U	S	A	A
R	E	B	A	R	P	N	N	A	R	K	G	N	O	S	Y
C	A	L	C	I	O	F	I	O	R	E	N	T	I	N	O
N	A	S	O	O	F	Y	M	I	R	S	A	A	D	P	F
D	Y	L	B	H	L	A	H	V	I	R	A	K	A	E	T
O	L	N	C	D	H	T	I	E	S	C	Y	I	N	R	H
B	L	A	E	O	E	C	P	C	R	I	S	Y	U	I	E
E	E	R	N	H	O	L	I	E	L	T	O	N	B	R	D
D	H	E	R	E	E	I	R	D	A	N	E	G	E	D	E
V	P	N	S	V	A	D	K	M	R	A	H	A	E	O	A
M	U	I	B	O	D	P	A	Z	C	L	M	N	N	N	D
G	A	I	C	E	A	N	D	S	N	O	W	A	L	M	O
M	C	S	N	A	I	D	N	I	I	A	D	T	U	H	N

Find the festival names hidden in the grid.

HOLI – is a Hindu festival celebrated in India. Colorful powder is thrown over people to celebrate the arrival of spring.

SONGKRAN – this festival in Thailand is held to mark the beginning of the New Year. People celebrate with water fights.

DAY OF THE DEAD – is held in Mexico in fall to remember relatives who have died.

ICE AND SNOW – in winter, residents of Harbin, China, build a whole city of ice.

UP HELLY AA – is a festival held on an island off the coast of Scotland. People dress up as Vikings, march in torch parades, and burn a Viking ship.

CALCIO FIORENTINO – is a soccer game held in Florence, Italy, played in period costume. Punching, wrestling, and kicking are allowed. The winning team wins a cow!

Can you spot the fake in this festival list?

- Floating lantern festival, Hawaii
- Hair-freezing festival, Yukon, Canada
- Dog-painting festival, Tokyo, Japan
- Underwater music festival, Florida, USA
- Mud festival, South Korea

GENIUS

1. Every summer in Spain, thousands of people celebrate La Tomatina, by gathering in the streets and throwing .... at each other.

a) tacos
b) tangerines
c) tomatoes

2. In Gloucestershire, England, people run after a whole .... as it is rolled down the scarily-steep slopes of Cooper's Hill.

a) cheese
b) cake
c) pineapple

Fill in the missing word in each sentence by choosing from the three options below.

3. In Lopburi, Thailand, 3,000 .... gather to dine on a buffet of fruit, vegetables, and ice cream.

a) cats
b) people
c) monkeys

4. In Spain, people line their .... up on a blanket, and a man dressed as the devil jumps over them.

a) purses
b) dogs
c) babies

125

BEAUTIFUL BUILDINGS

Some buildings are so unique that it seems impossible to believe they are real. Let's see if you have an eye for unusual architecture, or if you'll hit a brick wall with these questions.

NEWBIE

Can you match these world-famous buildings with their descriptions?

1. St. Basil's Cathedral
2. The Gherkin
3. Lotus Temple
4. St. Paul's Cathedral
5. Sagrada Familia
6. Petronas Towers

A) This Spanish basilica (large church) was designed by the architect Antoni Gaudi.

B) Towering over the skyline in Kuala Lumpur, these two towers are linked by a skybridge on the 41st and 42nd floors.

C) This London skyscraper's address is 30 St. Mary's Axe, but it is more often known by its foodie nickname.

D) This famous landmark in Russia is instantly recognizable thanks to its brightly colored domes.

E) This Indian temple is named after an exotic flower.

F) The gray dome of this London cathedral is one of London's most well-known sights.

ROOKIE

The Aalsmeer Flower Auction building in the Netherlands has the largest land area of any building in the world and sells 20 million flowers a day. It covers the same area as:

A) 6 soccer fields
B) 100 soccer fields
C) 28 soccer fields

GENIUS

Which of these materials has NOT been used to construct a building:

beer bottles, plastic bottles, newspaper, animal dung, Lego, cheese, mud, mammoth bones?

HAPPY TRAVELING!

There's nothing like getting away and exploring somewhere new. But when it comes to different destinations, have you got these sussed or are you completely lost?

NEWBIE

1. If you go here, you can live with the local Inuit, go dogsledding, and explore frozen caves.

A) The Amazon Rainforest, Brazil
B) Igloo village, Greenland
C) Niagara Falls, Canada

2. How about a trip to the poison garden? Be careful, as it's packed with deadly plants!

A) Alnwick, Northumberland, UK
B) Kew Gardens, London, UK
C) The Eden Project, Cornwall, UK

3. You could stay at the Panda Inn, which has a panda theme (of course), with panda furniture, art, and even the staff dressed up in panda outfits!

A) Sichuan, China
B) Wellington, New Zealand
C) Brussels, Belgium

4. If you enjoy a museum with a difference, how about one in a sewer? A stone's throw from one of Europe's most famous landmarks, this is the place to be to find out more about the history of processing, ahem, poop.

A) Paris, France
B) Rome, Italy
C) Orlando, USA

Read the descriptions and choose the correct destination.

5. At this underwater restaurant on a tropical island, fish will be swimming over your head rather than on the menu!

A) Oslo, Norway
B) The Maldives
C) Alaska, USA

ROOKIE

Unscramble the word to find out what's special about this hotel:

At the Das Park Hotel, in Linz, Austria, the rooms are made from EWERS pipes!

GENIUS

True or false?
Fifty years ago, an ice hotel was built in Norway and it still survives today!

COMMUNICATION SKILLS

Did you know that there are around 6,500 languages spoken in the world? So let's find out if you're a word nerd, or whether your language knowledge lets you down...

NEWBIE

Can you find 10 very rare languages in this word search?

A	L	R	E	B	R	T	A	N	E	M	A	S	O	A	T
K	R	C	I	M	O	K	R	S	L	L	H	A	N	A	N
A	S	H	I	O	R	I	H	S	U	A	T	J	J	G	S
L	E	A	A	A	Y	A	U	R	U	R	O	N	E	E	H
L	T	M	I	D	E	N	I	K	G	E	N	T	R	E	I
E	I	I	O	E	F	T	P	O	A	O	S	I	E	P	G
R	R	C	A	S	L	J	B	N	C	I	R	A	P	Y	A
F	D	U	M	I	E	G	U	G	B	C	X	I	O	A	T
H	O	R	Q	A	H	U	O	O	R	W	L	A	T	R	S
A	B	O	N	R	S	U	R	T	I	T	P	N	N	A	E
L	B	E	R	L	A	P	A	A	K	A	E	G	E	A	I
E	S	S	L	E	M	E	R	I	G	A	C	A	D	N	L
A	L	A	B	V	I	R	L	I	K	I	P	A	N	A	S
G	S	S	E	R	E	L	L	O	R	E	P	S	U	M	A
G	C	H	E	M	E	H	U	E	V	I	S	T	U	H	B

CHAMICURO – a language spoken by a handful of people in Peru

DUMI – spoken by a few people in Nepal

ONGOTA – an almost-extinct language spoken in parts of Ethiopia

LIKI – spoken on a few islands near Indonesia

TANEMA – spoken by very few people in the Solomon Islands

NJEREP – on the verge of extinction this language was once spoken in parts of Cameroon, Africa

CHEMEHUEVI – spoken by a few indigenous people in Colorado, USA

LEMERIG – only two people on the island of Vanuatu know this dialect

KAIXANA – a South American language that is almost extinct

TAUSHIRO – a language spoken in the Peruvian Amazon; almost extinct

ROOKIE

What is Esperanto?

A) a made-up international language to help people from different countries communicate

B) a language once spoken by people in Ancient Peru

C) a computer programming language

GENIUS

Which language was used by the Americans during World War II to send coded messages that wouldn't be decipherable by the enemy?

THE END OF LIFE

Like it or not, life is a one-way journey and it comes to an end for us all. B
death is marked in many different ways around the world. Do you know ho

NEWBIE

1. During Famadihana, what do the Malagasy people of Madagascar do?

A) take the bodies of their loved ones and wrap them in cloth, carrying them around the village
B) take food and gifts to their family graves to offer to their loved ones
C) honor their loved ones by placing their pictures on an altar and gathering together for an evening celebrating their lives and telling stories about them

2. For centuries in Tibet, loved ones have had sky burials. What does this mean?

A) that bodies were buried high on mountains
B) that bodies were cremated, then the ashes scattered to the sky
C) that bodies were taken to a mountaintop to decompose naturally

3. In Bolivia, people honor the dead on the "Day of Skulls" by:

A) decorating their skulls and having them blessed
B) painting pictures of their loved ones and placing them by their graves
C) giving money to the poor and sick

4. In parts of China, the coffins of loved ones are:

A) hung high on cliffs to keep them safe
B) placed in family tombs
C) given a burial at sea

5. The catacombs under the streets of Paris hold the remains of how many people?

A) 60,000
B) 600,000
C) 6 million

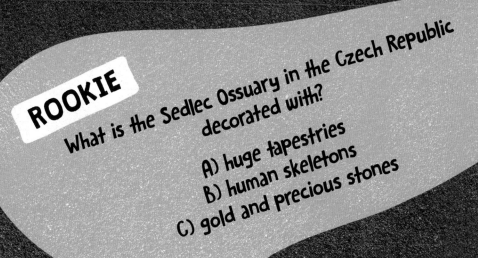

RAPID-FIRE QUESTIONS...

Our whirlwind round-the-world quiz is almost over. But before you see how you've done, here are a few rapid-fire questions, which could make all the difference to your score, so let's get cracking!

LARGE...

Will you be the best at answering questions on all things BIG?

NEWBIE

See if you can answer these true or false questions correctly:

1. Russia is the largest country on Earth.
2. The Great Wall of China can be seen from the moon.
3. The world's deepest mine in Mponeng, South Africa, is as deep as five Empire State Buildings stacked on top of each other.
4. Tokyo, Japan, covers more land than any other city in the world.
5. The largest highway in the world – the Katy Freeway in Texas, USA – has 26 lanes.

ROOKIE

Unscramble the anagram to finish the sentence:

The world's largest WNGIISMM OPLO, at San Alfonso del Mar resort in Chile, is so big that boats can sail it.

GENIUS

What's the largest living thing on Earth?

A) the elephant
B) the blue whale
C) the honey fungus

Which is the largest lake in the world?

A) Erie, B) Superior, C) Ontario

135

SMALL...

teeny-tiny and tricky, too!
How will you score on these questions?

NEWBIE

1. Which of these countries has the smallest coastline?

A) Monaco
B) Jordan
C) Slovenia

2. Vatican City is the world's smallest country. How many people live there?

A) 25
B) 800
C) 380

3. The Carmelit in Haifa, Israel, is the shortest subway system in the world. How long is it?

A) 1.6 miles (2.6km)
B) 1.1 miles (1.8km)
C) 0.2 miles (0.4km)

4. What size is the world's smallest flag?

A) half the size of a small sticky note
B) the size of a baby's fingernail
C) tenth the width of a human hair

5. Which of these is the world's thinnest tower?

A) Burj Khalifa, Dubai
B) Brighton i360, UK
C) One World Trade Center, USA

ROOKIE

The bee hummingbird is the smallest bird in the world. But which are smaller, males or females?

True or false?
The Kingdom of Talossa, the first micronation – an independent small country, or state – was actually a teenager's bedroom in Milwaukee, USA!

FAST...

Zoooooooom! You'll have to think quickly to answer these questions.

NEWBIE

1. Which is faster over a long distance, a cheetah or a pronghorn antelope?

2. Which car has the fastest top speed, the Bugatti Veyron or the Porsche 911?

3. What's the record speed for typing the letters of the alphabet?
A) 3.43 seconds
B) 6.15 seconds
C) 8.13 seconds

4. True or false? It's thought to be impossible to run the 100-meter dash in less than 10 seconds.

5. How fast did the first cars travel?
A) as fast as a person walking
B) as fast as a horse trotting
C) as fast as a cheetah running

ROOKIE

true or false?

Recently in South Africa, it was shown that it was faster for a racing pigeon to carry a memory stick of files than it was to send the files using broadband.

GENIUS

How many calculations can the world's fastest computer, the Sunway TaihuLight, do in a second?

A) a million
B) a billion
C) a quadrillion

LONG...

You don't have long to go until the end of this book, but can you answer these questions about the world's longest things?

NEWBIE

1. Which country has the longest coastline in the world?

A) Canada
B) Russia
C) China

2. How long is the world's longest nonstop flight?

A) 12 hours 40 minutes
B) 15 hours 35 minutes
C) 17 hours 15 minutes

3. How long was the world's longest freight train?

A) 4.5 miles (7.3km)
B) 2.1 miles (3.4km)
C) 1 mile (1.6km)

4. At 2,625 feet (800 m), the Central-Mid-Levels escalator and walkway system is the longest in the world, but where can you on ride it?

A) Japan
B) Hong Kong
C) South Africa

5. China's Three Gorges Dam is the longest in the world, at over 1.2 miles (2km). When it was built, how many villages were flooded?

A) 1,350
B) 26
C) 432

ROOKIE

true or false?
The longest beach in the world, Praia do Cassino Beach in Brazil, stretches for 62 miles (100km).

GENIUS

In which country is there an all-night festival on the longest day of the year, when people make floral crowns and dance around a maypole?

LIFE OF LUXURY...

NEWBIE

Can you prove you've got a wealth of knowledge about these mega-expensive items?

1. The world's most expensive hotel is the Hotel President Wilson in Geneva, Switzerland. How much does it cost for one night in its luxury Royal Penthouse Suite?

A) 600 Swiss francs
B) 6,000 Swiss francs
C) 60,000 Swiss francs

2. The world's most expensive car, the Koenigsegg CCXR Trevita, costs around US$4.8 million. What is the body coated in?

A) sapphire dust
B) diamond dust
C) gold dust

3. True or false?
The International Space Station is the most expensive thing ever constructed.

4. The company Apple Inc. was started by Steve Jobs, Steve Wozniak, and a third investor, who sold his shares in Apple shortly after it formed for a mere US$800. His shares would now be worth:

A) US$3.5 million
B) US$35 million
C) US$35 billion

5. A plane ticket from New York to Mumbai and back will usually cost around US$1,500. Unless you feel like reserving a swanky "penthouse in the sky," complete with your own butler and chef, which will cost you a cool:

A) US$23,000
B) US$17,000
C) US$76,000

ROOKIE

If you had to choose between 1 oz (28 grams) of platinum or 1 oz (28 grams) of gold, which one would be worth more?

GENIUS

Can you name the most expensive spice in the world?

EPIC ENDEAVORS

You're almost there! Time to go out with a bang. See how you can boost your score with these questions about brave explorers.

NEWBIE

Can you match the explorers with their incredible journeys?

1. Charles Darwin
2. Christopher Columbus
3. Roald Amundsen
4. Marco Polo
5. Ferdinand Magellan
6. Neil Armstrong
7. Dr. Livingstone

A) In 1911, this Norwegian explorer led the first expedition to reach the South Pole.

B) This American astronaut was the first man to set foot on the moon, in 1969.

C) This explorer from Venice is well-known for exploring Asia.

D) This Spanish explorer inspired the rhyme, "In 1492 .... sailed the ocean blue."

E) This Scottish doctor and missionary explored many parts of Africa. In 1855, he was the first European to see what's now known as Victoria Falls, which he named after Queen Victoria.

F) In 1831, this famous naturalist joined HMS *Beagle* and spent four years sailing the world, collecting plants, and observing wildlife.

G) This Portuguese explorer is known for being the first person to sail around the world.

ROOKIE

What did the first astronaut to set foot on the moon say as he stepped onto its surface?

A) That's one small step for man, one giant leap for mankind.
B) The Eagle has landed.
C) The surface is fine and powdery.

GENIUS

True or false? Every mountain in the world has been climbed.

ANSWERS
Score 1 point for each correct answer

SECTION 1 AMAZING LOCATIONS
pp8-9 Continent Conundrum
NEWBIE:

North America
Europe
Asia
Africa
South America
Oceania
Antarctica

ROOKIE: Asia
BONUS QUESTION: Oceania

GENIUS: Africa

pp10-11 Flying the Flag
NEWBIE: 1D, 2E, 3B, 4A, 5C

ROOKIE: true

GENIUS: Nepal – the flag is
shaped like two triangles,
one above the other.

pp12-13 Country Queries
NEWBIE:

```
C E A O I K A L I Y Q K F E Z M
I R C G A D G E S P A I N S I N
A I N O R W A Y I A N G U S A I
R E B A R Y N F A P K G N O S P
S G E R M A N Y O R E N T I N O
N I S O O F Y M I R S A A Y P B
D N L B H T A H V I R A K L E C
O A N C D H T I E S E C N A R F
E A E O E C P C R I L Y T I T
C B R N H D L I Y L T L N I R I
E B E R E E I A D A N E G E D A
E I N S F I N L A N D H A E O Z
R R I B O R P A Z C L P N N N F
G A E M O N I Z W T T U A L M O
M C S N A I D N I I A D T U H N
```

BONUS QUESTION: France

ROOKIE:
Canada – silk
Australia – the Great Wall
United Kingdom – the Forbidden City

Italy – the Terracotta Army
United States – giant pandas

GENIUS: China

pp14-15 Where on Earth...?
NEWBIE:
1A, 2E, 3B, 4D, 5C, 6G, 7F

ROOKIE:
False – it was a gift from France

GENIUS:
Giza, Egypt

pp16-17 Terrific Transportation
NEWBIE: red, yellow, gondola,
cycling, bullet

ROOKIE:
1. Paris – Metro
New York – Subway
London – Underground (or Tube)

2. B) Some stations are incredibly
beautiful with marble ceilings and
even chandeliers.

3. D) push people onto the trains
during rush hour

GENIUS: 5,772 miles (9,289km)

pp18-19 City Search
NEWBIE:

```
O U A O I K A N D E N V E R Z M
C P C G A D G E S K A I N S I N
S S A H A A G W D A L L A S A I
I A B A R Y N Y A P K G N O S P
C N Q R M A N O O R E N T I N O
N G S O D A L R I R S A A R P B
A T L A N T A K V I R A K L E N
R L O S A N G E L E S S N A R O
F E A I O E C P C R I L Y T I T
N F R N C D L I Y E L T T A E S
A B E R E A I O D A N E G E D O
S I N S V A G Y M R A H A E O B
R R I B O R P K Z C H I C A G O
G A E M O N I O W T T U A L M O
W A S H I N G T O N D C T U H N
```

ROOKIE: Tokyo
BONUS QUESTION: Japan

GENIUS: Washington, DC

pp20-21 Towering Places
NEWBIE: Months, Elevators,
Floors, twin, Glass

ROOKIE: A) The Shard

GENIUS: D) more than five

pp22-23 Outstanding Buildings
NEWBIE:
1B, 2D, 3B, 4C, 5C

ROOKIE: A) 775

GENIUS: C) 2,900

pp24-25 Getting Away From it All
NEWBIE:
1. A short break in Holland
2. On safari in Kenya
3. Diving in the Bahamas
4. Theme park in Florida
5. Camping in a national park in
Colorado

ROOKIE: D) 149mph (240kph)

GENIUS: B) put it in a secure
container

SECTION 2 EPIC EARTH

pp26-27 Incredible Places
NEWBIE:
1. Everest
2. Grand Canyon
3. Great Barrier Reef
4. Victoria Falls

ROOKIE:
1A, 2C, 3B

GENIUS:
Hanging Gardens of Babylon,
Great Pyramid of Giza
BONUS QUESTION:
the Great Pyramid of Giza

pp28-29 Cool Continents
NEWBIE: 1G, 2F, 3A, 4E, 5C, 6D, 7B

ROOKIE: true

GENIUS: true

pp30-31 Wade into Rivers
NEWBIE: 1A, 2C, 3D, 4A, 5D

ROOKIE: D) caught fire – 12 times!

GENIUS: B) a waltz

pp32-33 Conquering Mountains
NEWBIE:

```
M S G E L B R U S E N V A R Z I
C P V V A D G E S K A I R S I N
S G M E A W G W D A L L I S A I
I A V R R S N G G P K G N W S O
C N Q E M A N M O R V N T M N R
M G S S D A L R Z R I I A R P A
U T V T P R C S C I N A K L E J
R L D S A N N E L F S S D A R N
F E A I C E C P C R O L Y T I A
N F R N T D L I Y E N T T A E M
A B E S E D I O D E N A L I D I
S I R S V A G Y M R A H A E O L
R A I B O R P K Z C H I C A G I
C A E F O N I O W T T U A G M K
A C O N C A G U A M D C T U H D
```

ROOKIE: Mauna Kea

GENIUS: False – the tallest is Olympus Mons on Mars

pp34-35 Under a Waterfall
NEWBIE: 1. true, 2. False, 3. False

ROOKIE: 1E, 2C, 3A, 4B, 5D

GENIUS: B)

pp36-37 Exploring a Rainforest
NEWBIE:

```
M A D A G A S C A R N V A R Z N
C P A L A Y E R S K A I R S I I
S G M K A W G W D A L Z I S A S
I A P A P U A N E W G U I N E A
C O N S E R V A T I O N T M N B
M G S S D N L R Z R I I A R P R
U T V O O L C S D A I N T R E E
R L D Z A A N E L F S S R A R V
F F A I C C C P C R O L E O I I
N M R N T I L I Y E N T E A E R
A B E S E P I O D E N A S I D O
S I E S V O G Y M R A I A E O G
R A I B O R P K K C H I C A G N
C M O U N T K I N A B U L U M O
A C E N D A N G E R E D T U H C
```

ROOKIE: the Amazon rainforest

GENIUS: D) 2.5 million

pp38-39 Crossing Deserts
NEWBIE: 1B, 2. true, 3A

ROOKIE:
Sahara
Arabian
Atacama
Gobi
Mojave
Kalahari

GENIUS:
1. False, 2. False,
3. true, 4. False, 5. true

pp40-41 Dive into Lakes
NEWBIE:
1. Superior
Ontario
Huron
Erie
Michigan

2. C) Great Lakes

ROOKIE: 1. oldest, 2. million,
3. monsters, 4. desert, 5. float

GENIUS: d) 20%
BONUS QUESTION: False

pp42-43 Mind-blowing Nature
NEWBIE:
1. Wind
2. Pink
3. Move
4. Alien
5. Rocks

ROOKIE:
1B, 2B 3A, 4A, 5B

GENIUS:
c) Jelly Sandwich Cliffs

SECTION 3 ANIMAL MAGIC

pp44–45 Animal Mysteries
NEWBIE:
1. Crocodile
2. Lion
3. Snake
4. Penguin
5. Rabbit
6. Elephant

ROOKIE:
1B, 2A, 3A, 4B, 5A

GENIUS: true – for example, the wood frog!

pp46–47 Incredible Insects
NEWBIE: 1B, 2D, 3A, 4C, 5E

ROOKIE:
1. Wasp
2. Fleas
3. Ticks
4. Mosquito
5. Horsefly

GENIUS:
1B, 2B, 3A

pp48–49 Excellent Imitation
NEWBIE:
1. Bee
2. Stripes
3. Eye
4. Snake
5. Stick

ROOKIE: true

GENIUS: False

pp50–51 – Hide and Seek!
NEWBIE: The candy spider is the fake.

ROOKIE: False

GENIUS: False – scientists have discovered that the changes are actually caused by their mood and temperature.

pp52–53 Danger! Danger!
NEWBIE:

```
S P A E L E P H A N T P F E T M
I R C G A D G R S T G K H S I N
A G R I Z Z L Y B E A R U S G R
R E B A R Y K N A R K G N O E P
C T L I O N F I O R E N T I R O
N I S O O F Y M I A S A A C P B
G R E A T W H I T E S H A R K A
E A N C D H T K E B C Y I O R R
M O S Q U I T O C R I L Y C I B
E B R N H D L I E A T P N O R O
D B E R O E I R O L N E G D D C
V I N C V A D K N O A H A I O G
M R I B O D P A P P L P N L N N
G S E M A N I Z I T T U A E M I
C E S N A I D N H I A D T U H K
```

ROOKIE: A) the same length as a newborn baby

GENIUS: true

pp54–55 Perilous Poison
NEWBIE:
1E, 2B, 3A, 4C, 5D

ROOKIE: true

GENIUS: False. Mammals such as the duck-billed platypus, slow loris, and shrew can all give a venomous bite!

pp56–57 Strength in Numbers
NEWBIE: 1A, 2C, 3A, 4C, 5A

ROOKIE: 1B, 2B, 3A

GENIUS: False – the largest, which is known as a supercolony, stretches for 3,728 miles (6,000km) across Europe!

pp58–59 Mind-boggling Migration
NEWBIE: 1C, 2B, 3D, 4A, 5E

ROOKIE: true

GENIUS: C) 43,496 miles (70,000km) – almost twice around the world

pp60–61 You Scratch My Back...
NEWBIE: 1A, 2A, 3B, 4C, 5A

ROOKIE: False! We have tiny bacteria that live in our gut. They live off the food we eat and help us to digest it and stay healthy.

GENIUS: C) a parasite

SECTION 4 INTO THE DEEP

PP62–63 Sailing the Seven Seas
NEWBIE: False – it could take twice as long

ROOKIE: 1A, 2B, 3A, 4B, 5A

GENIUS: True

PP64–65 Reefs
NEWBIE: 1D, 2B, 3A, 4E, 5C

ROOKIE: True

GENIUS: On shipwrecks

PP66–67 Diving Down
NEWBIE:
1. Mariana
2. Pacific
3. Meters
4. Deep
5. Creatures

ROOKIE: 2) the clownfish is not found in deep waters

GENIUS: True

PP68–69 Ocean Giants
NEWBIE:

```
B L U E W H A L E N T P F E T M
K R C G W D G R S T G K H S I N
I S R I H S I F Y L L E J S G R
L E B A A Y A N A R K G N O E K
L T F I L R N I O G E N T I E R
E I S O E F T M I A S A R L P A
R R O A S L S B T C S R A Y Y H
W A N C H H Q K E B C H I O A S
H O S Q A H U O C R W L Y C R G
A B R N R S I I E N T P N O A N
L B E R K I D R I K N E G D T I
E I N C V F D F P O A H A I N L
M R I B O R P A P P L P N L A S
G S S E L A H W M R E P S E M A
G I A N T O C T O P U S T U H B
```

ROOKIE: False – it's actually as big as a car!

GENIUS: C) the size of a dinner plate

PP70–71 Danger in the Deep
NEWBIE: 1E, 2C, 3B, 4A, 5D

ROOKIE: Yes! Oceans are home to more than 60 species of sea snake.

GENIUS: Pufferfish, or "fugu" as the dish is known

PP72–73 Incredible Places
NEWBIE:
1. Waterfall
2. Seashells
3. Grotto
4. Pillars
5. Sandbars

ROOKIE: False – it's 984 feet (300 m) across and 259 feet (124 m) deep!

GENIUS: A) a tidal whirlpool

PP74–75 Ride the Waves
NEWBIE:

```
A L R E B R A L E O P P F O A M
K R C G W R G R S L L E W S I N
I S R I H S E F Y L L E J S G R
L E B A A Y A A R K G N O E K
M T T I D E N I K G E N T I E R
E I S O E F T M I E S A A L P H
R R O A S L S B T C R R A W Y H
K A N C R E S T E B C S I O A S
H O S Q A H U O C R W L Y T R F
A B R N R S U R F N T P N R A N
L B E R K I D R I K N E G E T I
E T S U N A M I P O A H A D N L
M R I B O R P A P P L P N N A S
G S S E R E L L O R E P S U M A
G I M N T O C B O P R S T U H B
```

ROOKIE: False – it's actually an incredible 78 feet (23.7 m)!

GENIUS: C) 14

PP76–77 Islands and Atolls
NEWBIE:
1. Greenland

ROOKIE:
1. True
2. True
3. False – it takes six
4. True
5. False – there are over 6,000

GENIUS: C) It has a prison that no one ever successfully escaped from.

PP78–79 Amazing Journeys
NEWBIE:
humpback whale
Adélie penguin
elephant seal
sardine
gray whale
tuna

ROOKIE: A) to lay eggs

GENIUS: B) seeds that are dispersed by the ocean

ANSWERS

SECTION 5 WHEN DISASTER STRIKES

PP80-81 Wild Weather
NEWBIE: A) cyclones, hurricanes, and typhoons

ROOKIE: B) Hurricane Patricia reached speeds of 202mph (325kph), almost the top speed of a Formula 1 racing car.

GENIUS:
1. Hurricane
2. Tornado
3. Hurricane
4. Tornado
5. Tornado
6. Hurricane

PP82-83 Scary Storms
NEWBIE: 1C, 2B, 3C, 4A, 5B

ROOKIE: False! It's actually around 1.2 million strikes a year!

GENIUS: C) Tamarack, California, with a record-breaking snowfall of 37.7 feet (11.5m) in 2011 - enough to bury the average two-story house.

PP84-85 Horrible Heatwaves
NEWBIE:

```
S P A G L E P H S N T P F E T M
I R C G A S U N S T G K H S I N
A G R I U Z I Y N E A R U T O H
R P B A R Y K N A R K G N O E P
C A L S C O R C H E D N T I R O
N R S U O F Y M I A S A A C P B
G C E M E W W I T E S F A R S H
E H N M D H T K E B C Y I G R F
K E B E U I T P C A I L Y C I B
E D R R H D L I E K T P N R R O
D B E R O E I R O I N E G D O I
V I N C V A D K P N A H A I O E
M R I B O D P A P G L P N L N N
G S T H G U O R D I T T U A E M I
C E S N A I D N H I A D T U H K
```

PP86-87 Terrible Earthquakes
NEWBIE:
1. Do, 2. Don't! 3. Do, 4. Do, 5. Don't!

ROOKIE: A) 2,000 years ago

GENIUS: False! Most happen along a U-shape in the Pacific Ocean, called the "Ring of Fire"

PP88-89 Fiery Volcanoes
NEWBIE: mountain, cone, lava, eruption, ash, smoke
BONUS QUESTION: The other words describe a beach.

ROOKIE: D) Australia

GENIUS: 1C, 2A, 3E, 4B, 5D

PP90-91 Mighty Floods
NEWBIE:
1. China
2. Flash
3. London
4. Deserts
5. Person

ROOKIE: B) the Netherlands

ROOKIE:
1. Dangerous fool
2. Keeping cool
3. Dangerous fool
4. Dangerous fool
5. Keeping cool
6. Dangerous fool
7. Keeping cool
8. Keeping cool
9. Keeping cool
10. Dangerous fool

GENIUS: D) 240 years

GENIUS: true

PP92-93 Terrifying Tsunamis
NEWBIE: 1) true , 2) false - only four have been, 3) true, 4) true, 5) true

ROOKIE: d) One World Trade Center, New York

GENIUS: D) 7 feet (2 m)

PP94-95 Slippery Avalanches and Mudslides
NEWBIE:

```
B L E B W H L W E T S A F E T M
K R C G W D G R S T G K H S I N
I S R I A V A L A N C H E S G R
L S B A A Y A N A R K G N O E B
L E L I L R S L O P E N T I E E
E A S I E F T M I S S A A L P A
G R O A D L S B T N S R A R Y C
W C N C H E Q K E I C H I C E O
H H S A N U O C A W L Y C R N
O B R N R S I I E T P N O A N
L B E R K N D R I N N E G D T I
E I N C V N O D F P U A H A I N K
M R I B O W P A P O L P N L A S
G S S E L A H W M M E P S E M A
G I E U C S E R O P U P T U H B
```

ROOKIE: C) less than a minute

GENIUS: Yes. In 1618, the Swiss village of Plurs was completely destroyed by an avalanche.

PP96-97 Blazing Wildfires
NEWBIE: All of the things listed can start a wildfire.

ROOKIE: D) 7.5mph (12kph) - about the same pace as a human running

GENIUS: True! Some plants need fires to release their seeds, and the ash from the fire also makes the soil fertile.

SECTION 6 EXTREME PLACES

pp98–99 The Arctic
NEWBIE: 1. kangaroo, 2. outback,
3. heatwave, 4. swimsuit,
5. Sydney
BONUS QUESTION: Australia

ROOKIE: C) No one knows for sure
if it was Peary or Cook.

GENIUS: Humans – global warming
is destroying Arctic ice and the
habitats of the wildlife.

pp100–101 The Antarctic
NEWBIE: 1) fact, 2) fact, 3) fib,
4) fib, 5) fact, 6) fib, 7) fib,
8) fact

ROOKIE: Snorkel

GENIUS: A) five minutes, tops

pp102–103 Most Dangerous Roads
NEWBIE: 1D, 2C, 3E, 4A, 5A

ROOKIE: Permit

GENIUS: True!

pp104–105 Driest Places
NEWBIE: 1. Fact, 2. Fake, 3. Fact,
4. Fake, 5. Fact

ROOKIE: 1D, 2C, 3B, 4E, 5A

GENIUS: B) enough to fill 75
bathtubs

pp106–107 Highest Places in the World
NEWBIE:

```
A L R E B R A L E O P P F O A M
X R C I M O K R S L L H A S A N
I S R I H S E F Y L L E J S G S
L E E A A Y A U R U R O N O E H
T L I D E N I K G E N T I E I
I I A O E F T P O T O S I L P G
R R L A S L J B T C R R A W Y A
J A T C R E S U E B C S I O A T
H O O Q A H U O L R W L Y T R S
A B R N R S U R F I T P N R A E
L B E R L A P A Z R A E G E T I
E T S U N A M I P O A C A D N L
L E A D V I L L E P L A N A S
G S S E R E L L O R E P S U M A
G I M L A Y A B O P R S T U H B
```

ROOKIE: C) cable car

GENIUS: A) ascend slowly
over several days so the body
acclimatizes
BONUS QUESTION: true

pp108–109 Most Polluted Places to Live
NEWBIE: 1. Trees, 2. Laundry,
3. Earth, 4. Smog, 5. Nuclear

ROOKIE: true

GENIUS: Antarctica

pp110–111 Most Remote Settlements
NEWBIE:

```
A L R E B R A L E O P R Y O D M
K R C I M O K R S L L A A S A N
I E A S T E R F Y L L O J S G S
E T L G I L B E R T E L T I E I
I B A O E F T P F T O S I C P G
R R E A S L J B A C R R A O Y A
A A T A R E S U R B E S I C A D
U O O Q R H U O O R G L Y O R L
Q B R N R S U R E I R P N S A I
C B E R L A P A S K O E G E T K
A T S U N A M I P O E C A D N T
M P I T C A I R N P G P A N A S
G S S E R E L L O R T P S U M A
G I M L S Y A B O P S T U H B
```

ROOKIE: False. It was 81 days!

GENIUS: A) by mule

pp112–113 Most Crowded Places to Live
NEWBIE: Manila, the Philippines

ROOKIE: 1E, 2D, 3B, 4C, 5A

GENIUS: D) 1,200

pp114–115 Wettest Places
NEWBIE:
1. true
2. False – they fell more than 1.6
billion years ago!
3. False – they can reach speeds
of 22mph (35kph)
4. true
5. true

ROOKIE: A) 85 feet (26 m) –
almost the height of a nine-story
building!

GENIUS: C) petrichor

SECTION 7 STRANGE BUT TRUE

pp116–117 Peculiar Places
NEWBIE: 1. Real, 2. Real, 3. Real, 4. Real, 5. Real, 6. Real, 7. Fake, 8. Fake, 9. Real, 10. Real, 11. Fake, 12. Fake, 13. Fake, 14. Real, 15. Real

ROOKIE: Trick question alert! All of these are correct.

GENIUS: C) 1
BONUS QUESTION: Y in France, or Å in Norway.

pp118–119 Manners Matter
NEWBIE: 1F, 2B, 3E, 4D, 5C, 6A

ROOKIE: A) by burping loudly

GENIUS: Yes! It's illegal in Singapore.

pp120–121 the Whole Truth?
NEWBIE:
1. Lies, 2.Lies, 3. true, 4. Lies, 5. true, 6. true, 7. Lies, 8. true, 9. Lies, 10. true

ROOKIE: Blindfolded

GENIUS: true

pp122–123 World's Strangest Jobs
NEWBIE:
1. Pet food
2. Worms
3. Snakes
4. Fortune cookie
5. Hackers

ROOKIE: true

GENIUS: B) tea caddy – this is actually a small tin used to store tea!

pp124–125 Fabulous Festivals
NEWBIE:

```
C E A O I K A L I Y Q K F E Z M
I R C G A S G E S T G J H S I D
A I A H A A G J I A N G U S A Y
R E B A R P N N A R K G N O S Y
C A L C I O F I O R E N T I N O
N A S O O F Y M I R S A A D P F
D Y L B H L A H V I R A K A E T
O L N C D H T I E S C Y I N R H
B L A E O E C P C R I S Y U I E
E E R N H O L I E L T O N B R D
D H E R E E I R D A N E G E D A
V P N S V A D K M R A H A E O A
M U I B O D P A Z C L M N N N O
G A I C E A N D S N O W A L M O
M C S N A I D N I I A D T U H N
```

ROOKIE: Dog-painting festival!

GENIUS: 1C, 2A, 3C, 4C

pp126–127 Beautiful Buildings
NEWBIE: 1D, 2C, 3E, 4F, 5A, 6B

ROOKIE: B) 100 soccer fields

GENIUS: Cheese

pp128–129 Happy Traveling!
NEWBIE: 1B, 2A, 3A, 4A, 5B

ROOKIE: Sewer

GENIUS: False – a new ice hotel is built every winter.

pp130–131 Communication Skills
NEWBIE:

```
A L R E B R T A N E M A S O A T
K R C I M O K R S L L H A N A N
A S H I O R I H S U A T J J G S
L E A A A Y A U R U R O N E E H
L T M I D E N I K G E N T R E I
E I I O E F T P C A O S I E P G
R R C A S L J B N C I R A P Y A
F D U M I E G U G B C X I O A T
H O R Q A H U O O R W L A T R S
A B O N R S U R T I T P N N A E
L B E R L A P A A K A E G E A I
E S S L E M E R I G A C A D N L
A L A B V I R L I K I P A N A S
G S S E R E L L O R E P S U M A
G C H E M E H U E V I S T U H B
```

ROOKIE: A) a made-up international language to help people from different countries communicate

GENIUS: Navajo – a Native American language

pp132–133 the End of Life
NEWBIE: 1A, 2C, 3A, 4A, 5C

ROOKIE: B) Human skeletons

GENIUS: the moon – the remains of Dr. Eugene Shoemaker were carried there by *Lunar Prospector* in 1999.

SECTION 8 RAPID-FIRE QUESTIONS...

pp134–135 Large...
NEWBIE:
1. True
2. False
3. False – it's actually a little deeper than 10 Empire State Buildings!
4. False – it's New York
5. True

ROOKIE: Swimming pool

GENIUS: C) the honey fungus
BONUS QUESTION: B) Superior

pp136–137 Small...
NEWBIE:
1. A
2. B
3. B
4. C
5. B

ROOKIE: Males

GENIUS: True

pp138–139 Fast...
NEWBIE:
1. A pronghorn
2. The Bugatti Veyron
3. A
4. False. Usain Bolt has run the 100-meter dash in 9.58 seconds.
5. A

ROOKIE: True!

GENIUS: C) a quadrillion

pp140–141 Long...
NEWBIE:
1. A
2. C
3. A
4. B
5. A

ROOKIE: False! It is 158 miles (254km) long!

GENIUS: Sweden

pp142–143 Life of Luxury...
NEWBIE:
1. C
2. B
3. True!
4. C
5. C

ROOKIE: 1 oz (28 grams) of platinum

GENIUS: Saffron

pp144–145 Epic Endeavors
NEWBIE: 1F, 2D, 3A, 4C, 5G, 6B, 7E

ROOKIE: A) That's one small step for man, one giant leap for mankind.

GENIUS: False – Gangkar Punsum in Bhutan is the world's 40th-highest peak, but climbing it has been banned for religious reasons.

COLORING YOUR MAP

Hopefully you've been keeping score as you make your way through the sections. Once you earn enough points, you can color a continent on the world map on pages 156–157. There are eight levels to pass – the more questions you answer, the faster you will color your map.

The levels for coloring each continent are shown in the box opposite. Your first target is to reach 40 points, then you can color Europe. See if you can make it all the way to 475 points! Once you're finished, there's a certificate at the back of the book for you to cut out and display on your wall.

TOP SCORE

Europe .... 40 points

North America .... 90 points

South America .... 140 points

Africa .... 200 points

Asia .... 270 points

Oceania .... 320 points

Antarctica .... 400 points

The Oceans .... 475 points

MAP TO COLOR

Choose some bright colors for your continents – remember to save blue for when you hit the 475 mark so you can color the oceans!

Atlantic Ocean

Pacific Ocean

South America

Remember – if you are playing against your family and friends, make some copies of the map before you start!

Arctic Ocean

Europe

Asia

Africa

Pacific Ocean

Indian Ocean

Oceania

Southern Ocean

Antarctica

157

CONGRATULATIONS!

You've finished the quiz. Add your name and your score to the certificate and carefully cut it out to put on your wall.

....

has successfully completed the Round-the-World Quiz Book with an amazing score of

....

WELL DONE!

Date: ....